MAKE TOONS That SELL

without selling out!

by

Bill Plympton

"the King of Indie Animation"

Routledge
Taylor & Francis Group

LONDON AND NEW YORK

First published 2012

This edition published 2015 by Focal Press

Published 2017 by Routledge
2 Park Square, Milton Park, Abingdon, Oxon OX14 4RN
711 Third Avenue, New York, NY 10017, USA

First issued in hardback 2017

*Routledge is an imprint of the Taylor & Francis Group,
an informa business*

Library of Congress Cataloging-in-Publication Data
Plympton, Bill.
  Make 'toons that sell without selling out : the Bill Plympton
    guide to independent animation success / by Bill Plympton.
    pages cm
  Includes bibliographical references and index.
  ISBN 978-0-240-81779-8 (alk. paper)
  1. Animated films—Vocational guidance. 2. Animation
(Cinematography)—Vocational guidance. I. Title.
  NC1765.P58 2012
  741.5'8—dc23
  2011053080

British Library Cataloguing-in-Publication Data
A catalogue record for this book is available from the British
Library.

ISBN-13: 978-1-138-40306-2 (hbk)
ISBN-13: 978-0-240-81779-8 (pbk)

PREFACE

Where did you get your talent?

Back in my twenties, when I was a struggling illustrator in New York, things weren't going so well – no one liked my artwork, my syndicated strip was going badly, it was in only twenty newspapers, and they were diminishing. Any time I tried to create a cartoon that I felt was hard-hitting, the newspaper editors thought it was offensive and in bad taste.

At that point, it felt like my career was a big flop. I could barely pay my rent, my meals consisted of ramen noodles and popcorn, and my landlord (who worked at a fabric store on the ground floor) made it very difficult for me to get in and out of my apartment without him yelling "Pay the damn rent!" at me.

Consequently, I had to spend my days wandering around the city or going to movies all day, in order to avoid any confrontation with my landlord. What was I going to do? Get a normal job? Even though I'd graduated from college with an art degree, I was totally untrained and unprepared for any other kind of normal profession. Besides, I loved walking around the city, proudly carrying my black leather portfolio that subtly suggested, "There goes a professional artist, an *illustrator*! Someone who'd just done the current cover of the *New Yorker* or *Vanity Fair*, no doubt!" I was just one tiny step away from Cindy Crawford or Claudia Schiffer, who also carried around black leather portfolios and appeared on magazine covers.

I could always call it quits and return to Oregon as an artistic failure. Maybe I could sneak back to my hometown in the middle of the night so no one would notice. But I liked New York City. I loved the excitement, the variety, the weirdness – I didn't want to leave.

I was in a total funk. I decided to walk the streets of this mad city and ponder my next move. As I exited onto the bustling East Village Street, my landlord yelled at me for the thousandth time: "Hey, Plympton, the rent!" But I ignored him. After all, if I did decide to vacate the Big Rotten Apple, paying the rent would be a moot point.

I wandered the late-evening streets; the sun was about to set. I had no idea where I was or where I was going – I was a sleep-walking zombie. As it started getting darker, I realized that I was lost. New York is a very easy city in which to find one's way because most of the streets are numbered – tourists love that! But the street signs around me were no help at all – as far as I could tell, I was at the corner of "Nowhere" and "Eternity."

But that wasn't the only strange observation. As I looked around me, the streets were deserted – which by itself is not too rare a condition for certain neighborhoods at that time of night – but I mean not a single living thing. No people, cops, pets, birds – nothing.

To top it off, all of the apartments seemed abandoned. There was no advertising, no decorations, no signs of human culture anywhere – I felt like I was on a Hollywood backlot, after hours. Oddly, I wasn't concerned – it wasn't like I had any pressing meetings or art deadlines to meet. Actually, I was kind of digging the surrealism of the moment. But wait: it got even more bizarre.

I noticed an object flying straight at me out of the golden glow of the setting sun. It was hard to make out at first because of the solar glare – was it a large bird? A plane? As it got closer, I realized it was some guy

riding on a missile – kind of like the last scene in *Dr. Strangelove*, when Slim Pickens rode the nuclear missile right into the destructive mushroom cloud explosion.

But what really blew my mind was that the guy flew right up to me and parked his missile in front of me. Then I realized that it would have been more normal if it were Mr. Pickens – instead, it was a bright red naked man with horns, riding on a #2 Ticonderoga pencil.

Okay, I know that I live in the weirdest city in the world, but this appearance crossed even my weirdness threshold – I stood smack in the middle of the intersection of "Twisted" and "Strange" streets.

Dear readers, I know you're getting very impatient with this absurd story and you'd like me to get on with my tips for animation success. So I'll just paraphrase what took place on that magical NYC evening. In his raspy voice, the man offered me a way out of my career dilemma. He had a deal for me, and the deal sounded quite good. As I recall, it was something about how I could be a great success in the cartoon business, but he wanted two things in return.

I was pretty much down on my luck, and I was open to any kind of offer at that point. His offer was this. Point one – he wanted me to change from print cartoons to animation. Point two – he wanted my eternal soul! Okay, big problem – although I loved animation (as a kid, Daffy Duck was my favorite character), I had absolutely no idea how to make animated cartoons. But he replied that this was no problem – he'd snap his fingers and I'd magically know everything there was to know about animation.

"That's cool!" I said. "Let's do it!"

The hovering pencil quickly came alive, and his body turned into a giant red hand, guiding the pencil as it drew some kind of sketch, right there in midair. The hand was definitely that of a quick sketch artist, and the sketch looked just like me! What happened next almost defies description – I know what I've stated already pushes the limits of credibility, but this was the crème de la crème of bizarre – the sketched doppelganger came to life and walked into my body! Then the giant flying Ticonderoga pencil put its graphite point into my heart, and I heard a ghoulish, cold wind sound, as if I were taking my last breath.

Just then, a manhole cover blew sky high with a loud bang, and flames erupted from underneath the pavement. The bright red man on the #2 pencil swirled around and flew down into the opening and under the city streets with a great shaking and thunder like an earthquake. Then silence settled over that deserted intersection. It took me about 30 seconds to regain my breathing, and then suddenly that desolate street was filled with people – the buildings came to life with ads and signs, and it became a normal neighborhood … odd!

As I skipped home with a new sense of optimism and excitement about my now-prosperous future, visions of success swept through my imagination: women, money, power, prizes, accolades, red carpets, and fancy film festivals. It was a dizzying walk home, and as I bounded up my apartment stairway, the door was blocked by Mr. Landlord. I brushed by him, exclaiming, "Your wait is over, I'm going to be a big cartoon star!"

As I disappeared behind my apartment door, he yelled, "You're not a star, but you're certainly a cartoon!" And that's how I became the rock star of animation.

Okay, so maybe it didn't happen exactly that way, but part of it is true. In animation, anything can happen, and the only limits are those of the animator's imagination. And I hope this book can be your magical Ticonderoga to success.

No one is born to be anything – except maybe for royalty. People often say to me, "You were born to be an artist." I wasn't born to be anything – I worked my proverbial ass off. If I were to offer any reason for my so-called success, it's that I freaking love to draw. I wake up in the morning fantasizing about what I'm going to draw that day, and at the end of the day, I feel so happy that I've spent the day at my drawing board creating characters.

People call me a masochist for drawing a whole film by myself, but I think I'm a hedonist!

Just beware of naked red men riding on Ticonderoga #2 pencils!

ACKNOWLEDGMENTS

I want to thank numerous people for their invaluable and generous help in putting this book together.

First of all, John Holderried, who faithfully transcribed my gibberish scribblings into copy that actually makes sense.

Sara Ho, who helped shape the book into the graphically interesting form you now have in your hands.

Everyone in my studio: Lindsay Woods, Desirée Stavracos, and Sandrine Flament. Also, everyone at Focal Press. Thank you for your immense help.

My book agent, Jim Fitzgerald. Also, the contributing artists: Don Hertzfeldt, Peter Lord, Pat Smith, Marv Newland, Greg Ford, Signe Baumane, Cordell Barker, Winsor McCay, Pink Martini, Nicole Renaud, Alex Tiedtke, and Martha Plimpton.

–Bill Plympton

CONTENTS

Chapter 1   Introduction   1

The Second Golden Age of Animation   2

Chapter 2   My History   7

Early Influences   8

Humor in School   11

Oregon's Climate   12

The Big Apple   16

Print Cartoons   18

"Your Face"   20

Chapter 3   Making an Animated Film   23

Raising the Money   25

Idea   25

Synopsis (Storyboard)   27

Budget   28

Marketing Plan   30

Concept Art   34

Title   35

Grants   35

Family and Friends   36

Hollywood   36

Kickstarter and Internet   37

Self-Investment   39

Plympton's Dogma   40

Dogma Point #1: Make Your Film *Short*   40

Dogma Point #2: Make Your Film *Cheap!*   41

Dogma Point #3: Make the Film *Funny*   41

Alternative Funding   43

Chapter 4   Production   47

Creating a Studio   48

Chapter 5   Storytelling   53

The Myth of Story   54

Intuition   55

Conflict   57

Other Directors' Notes   58

Don Hertzfeldt ("Rejected", "Billy's
Balloon")   58

Peter Lord (Aardman's *Chicken Run*):   58

Pat Smith ("Mask", "Delivery")   58

Comedy   61

Character Development   66

Children versus Adults   68

Live Action versus Animation   70

Censorship versus Self-Censorship   71

Chapter 6   Character Design   73

Strong Personality   77

Dynamic Shapes   77

Simplicity   79

Line of Action   80

Pushing the Eye Around   89

What Not to Do   90

Chapter 7   Storyboarding   93

Chapter 8   Voices   99

Casting   101

Chapter 9   Animation   109

Influences   110

Techniques   112

Animation Secrets   113

Caricatures   116

The Human Body   121

The Face	125
Design	132
Silhouettes	134
Previz	135
Walk Cycles	137
Point of View	138
Perspective and Foreshortening	140
Distortion	143
Shadows	144
Metamorphosis	145
Pencil Test	146
Backgrounds	150
Perfectionism	152
Digitizing the Art	158
Scanning	158
Cleaning	159
Color	159
Compositing	160

Chapter 10   Postproduction — 163

Editing	164
Timing	165
Conflict	167
Effects	168
Humor	169
Reviewing the Film	172
Sound	172
Real versus Cartoony Sound	174
Dolby	175
Music	175
Ironic Music	177
Music Budgeting	178
How to Save Money	179
Film Composers	183
Music Clearances	184
Testing	185

Chapter 11   Selling Your Film — 189

Market Festivals	194
Fun Festivals	196
Comic Conventions	198
How to Find the Right Festival	199
The Tune Deal	202
The *Strange Person* Deal	203
Telluride Story	204
The Distribution Deal	205
Distributor Complaints	206

Chapter 12   Self-Distribution   **209**

Booking the Theatre   210

Personal Touch   211

Nontheatrical   211

Press Agent   212

Guerilla Publicity   212

TV Spots   214

Television   214

Ownership   216

Mini-Disney   216

DVD   217

Piracy   218

VOD   218

Merchandise   219

Personal Appearances   221

Commissioned Work   222

Music Videos   223

Chapter 13   Advice to Young Animators   **225**

Finding the Right School   226

What to Study in School   227

After School   228

Afterword   **233**

Index   **235**

Chapter 1

INTRODUCTION

Bill Plympton

The Second Golden Age of Animation

You students today are extremely fortunate to be living in a time that many people refer to as the Second Golden Age of Animation. You should now bend down and kiss your Wacom tablet, laptop, computer workstation, or whatever you use to create cartoons in eternal thanks for being born in a blessed time for animators. As for myself, I will kiss my ancient wooden drawing table and light box.

The First Golden Age of Animation lasted from around 1930 to 1956 and pretty much coincided with Walt Disney's rise to power, but then Walt got bored and directed his energies to television, live action, and theme parks.

In my opinion, this era created some of the most wonderful characters ever: Mickey Mouse, Goofy, Popeye, Betty Boop, Bugs Bunny, Daffy Duck, the Road Runner—and great films: *Snow White and the Seven Dwarfs, Bambi, Song of the South, Dumbo,* "Red Hot Riding Hood," and "The Great Piggy Bank Robbery."

Jobs in animation were plentiful. Because no one studied animation in school and there were no graduate programs, most early animators were political or humor cartoonists looking for extra money. Suddenly, because of Disney, these part-time cartoonists became superstars, going from studio to studio and project to project, and each time they changed jobs, they got a big bump in pay—kind of like today's superstar athletes.

However, for many reasons, the period from the late 1950s to the 1980s became the Death Valley of animation. I think the prominence of TV animation killed off the great cartoons. All of the Hanna-Barbera and Rankin/Bass series showed that animation didn't have to cost as much or use as many great artists. Also, movie theaters decided to cut back on showing short films before the main features. So all of this great reservoir of talent were forced to either retire or work on Hanna-Barbera's crap.

MTV LOGO: ART FOR MTV 10 SECOND PROMOTION, COLOR PENCIL, 1988

Things then mysteriously changed. For some strange reason, by the mid-1980s, animation started to wake up. The art form finally passed through the arid desert of TV cartoons and arrived in the lush valley of the Second Golden Age of Animation. I believe it was just a happy accident that all of these great influences came together in just a few short years.

MTV started showing animation in the 1980s; *Who Framed Roger Rabbit?* was a huge hit. Japanese animation, including *Akira* and Hayao Miyazaki's films, started to invade American shores. The Disney studio decided to get back into animation with films such as *The Little Mermaid* and *The Rescuers Down Under*, which were both moneymakers. And of course, *The Simpsons* showed that TV animation could be biting and controversial—and not just for kids.

I believe one main reason for this huge animation revival was an audience ready for an art form that took their minds into a whole new realm of imagination. After years of true-to-life, hard-core, politically relevant films, the audience was ready for magic and fantasy, and animation was the only art form that could take the viewer to different worlds so easily—luckily for you, dear readers, because animation is now ubiquitous and extremely profitable. In 2010, five of the top ten grossing films were animated: *Toy Story 3*, *Despicable Me*, *Shrek Forever After*, *How to Train Your Dragon*, and *Tangled*.

Animation studios are starting up all over the world—India and China are making a big push to overtake the United States in animation production, and France and Germany are putting government funds into animation production. Everyone all over the world sees the financial success of Pixar, DreamWorks, and Blue Sky Studios, and they want to emulate these studios' stupendous profits.

What does this mean for young animators looking for work? *Money!* Not just jobs, but opportunities to create stories that are different, exciting, and moving. And that's what this book is about: how you can be part of this never-ending (I hope) explosion of animated cartoons. This book, I believe, will ably prepare you to be a creative and successful participant in the Second Golden Age of Animation.

why do you make Animation?

This question may be the most important one in this book. I do a lot of press interviews, but I'm never asked this question: "Why do I make animation?" I believe that a person's answer to this question has a great bearing on his or her success or failure. There are numerous answers; in fact, there are almost as many possible answers as there are animators: money, awards, approval from family and friends, stardom, self-esteem, creative outlet, childhood fantasy, and so on. They're all valid reasons.

But I will now give you *my* (numerous) answers:

1. Boredom—I find it very entertaining and amusing to create cartoons; it keeps life interesting.

2. Fear—Fear of failure, poverty, and unemployment. A wasted life.

3. The sound of laughter—I love making people laugh; it gives me a great feeling, knowing that I'm responsible for people's enjoyment.

4. Playing God—The high I get from spending all day creating whole worlds from my imagination.

There are other reasons, of course, but those are the main ones.

I often talk to students who believe that once they get a job at Pixar, they'll be rock-star rich. That's fine, but I'm not really in it for the money. In fact, I make my own sandwiches for lunch—I'm not a gourmet, just give me food to keep me drawing; all of my clothes are secondhand; I don't have a car; and I don't do drugs—all of my profits go into my next feature film.

For me, the biggest reason is that I love to draw! I sometimes draw all day, from 6:00 in the morning to 10:00 at night—and after these all-day sessions, I feel great! Refreshed! Like that was the best day of my life! I'm reborn! I don't exactly know why, but to me drawing is an exercise in self-discovery—I'm trying to see how good I can get and to experiment with how interesting I can make my drawings and my story.

Gourmets are obsessed with what they put into their mouths—I love what goes into my eyes; you could call me a visual gourmand.

I think that if I were ever arrested (though I can't imagine what for) and thrown in jail, I would thrive there. I'd finally have some peace and quiet to draw my films. If I did a five-year stretch, I'd emerge from prison with two feature films completed—how cool is that? I'd be the happiest guy in prison.

In fact, I'm so obsessed with the pencil that I fantasize that I will die because of the pencil. I plan out little scenarios of my death. Perhaps I'll be drawing such long hours that I fall asleep at the drawing board, and my head falls to the table, with the sharp end of the pencil piercing my eye and going into my brain.

Or perhaps I'll be walking across my studio, I won't see the pencil on the floor, I'll step on it, my feet will slip out from under me, and I'll crack my skull on my art table. Or after working late one night in bed, I'll fall asleep and roll over, piercing my heart with a discarded pencil.

Ironic, isn't it? It's like they say: "You live by the pencil, you die by the pencil."

Chapter 2
MY HISTORY

Early Influences

My earliest memory of animation—and remember, this was many years ago, and I don't have a photographic memory—is watching cartoons on TV at the age of 5.

I loved the craziness, the surrealism, and the humor of Bugs Bunny, Daffy Duck, and Popeye. Then along came the Disney shows—*The Wonderful World of Disney* and *The Mickey Mouse Club*. (I was a card-carrying member.)

I'm always amazed at the huge influence Walt Disney has had on our culture. If he had only created Mickey Mouse, that would be huge, but he also pioneered animated features and paved the way for the Pixar, DreamWorks, and Blue Sky films of today. He was also one of the first to show how merchandising can significantly increase a studio's income.

His studio was the first to move full force into television, at a time when all of the other film studios were deathly afraid of electronic media. And, of course, he was the guy who reinvented and reinvigorated amusement parks. Plus, he knew how to synthesize all of these elements—TV, films, amusement parks, merchandising—into building a huge brand of cartoons and fantasy. Mr. Walt Disney gets my vote as the greatest entertainer of the twentieth century.

So I would draw from memory all of these cartoon characters that I loved so much. But I never had enough paper, and I was forced to steal old envelopes and typing paper from my folks to draw on.

I remember one time very clearly—I must have been around 7 or 8—when my dad gave me one of those phone notepads that was about 4 × 3 inches because I was always running out of paper. I was so excited! Finally, I could draw everything I wanted and never run out of paper! (There were about 100 sheets in the pad.)

So I started with the simple things—cars, trucks, airplanes, houses, animals, trees—and then I got to people, and I realized that there weren't enough sheets of paper for all my planned drawings. "Wow," I thought, "I'm going to need a lot more of these notepads."

ME AT THE AGE OF 10 WITH MY
BIRTHDAY PRESENT, A PAINT SET

A SKETCH OF MY DAD (MADE WHEN
I WAS 15)

Finally, my folks realized that this cartoon habit I had was something serious—a phase that I was never going to outgrow—so they figured they might as well use it to keep me out of trouble. They started buying me stuff like an easel, a paint set, a palette, paper, a drawing board, a pencil sharpener, and other supplies.

I was so excited about creating art that I didn't know which direction would be the best for me. I loved cartoons, so maybe I'd work for Uncle Walt. I loved the Sunday funnies, so maybe I'd be like Charles Schulz of *Peanuts* fame. I loved spot gags, so maybe I'd do cartoons for the *New Yorker*, like Charles Addams.

I loved drawing cars, so maybe I'd move to Detroit and draw the cars of tomorrow. I loved painting, so maybe I'd move to New York and become a bohemian painter. I loved illustration, so maybe I'd study at the Art Center in Los Angeles and become an illustrator for the *Saturday Evening Post*, like Norman Rockwell.

Which direction to take my budding art talent? It was a tough decision for a kid, but there were two things that influenced my decision to become an animator.

My folks were very outgoing; they loved to party, and their parties were legendary. Sometimes, late at night when I was supposed to be in bed, I'd sneak up the stairs and spy on the wild party. My dad was usually the center of attention because he was so damn funny.

I marveled at how he was able to keep everyone's attention with his antics and jokes—wouldn't it be great if I were able to amuse people like that some day? That would be the best job in the world!

The second event that directed my career happened when I spotted the Preston Blair book *Animation* in my local department store. I'd never heard of Mr. Blair before, though I'd certainly seen his work on TV (Disney and MGM cartoons), and that book changed my life.

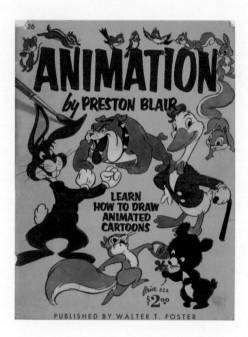

The way he used a pencil to create emotion, movement, and humor in the book showed me how the cartoons I'd seen on TV were made and how anyone who could draw could also make cartoons. Wow—what a revelation! I'd always imagined that Walt Disney drew all the cartoons himself, and there was no way I could replace the great Mr. Disney.

I remember watching a 1941 Disney feature called *The Reluctant Dragon* on TV in the mid 1950s; included with the film was footage of Robert Benchley going behind the scenes at the studio to see how animated films were made. There they were, right before my eyes: the animators! These are the guys that create the funny drawings! This is what I want to do—that's the job for me!

And once Mr. Blair's book showed me those secrets, hot damn: I was going to be an animator! My direction was clear; my goal was set. Next I had to study the greats by watching as many cartoons as possible to see how the magic was created. Even though I lived way out in the country far away from movie cinemas, art galleries, or museums, I took to hoarding anything that had to do with animation. I remember saving a *Saturday Evening Post* article from the early 1960s about Walt Disney. I bought Bugs Bunny and Donald Duck comics to study the art and stories.

I became a big fan of Charles Addams—I admired how he used people's pain, death, and suffering as a source of humor. How could he do that? We're supposed to feel sorry for people in pain. He was the father of so-called sick humor or dark humor that's so popular in the films and cartoons we see today.

And, of course, the Road Runner cartoons from Warner Bros. took a lot of that dark, violent humor and made me laugh. But it was Bugs Bunny and Daffy Duck that made me laugh the most. You can see their jokes and humor reflected in my cartoons.

Certainly, I loved the cartoons of the Fleischer brothers (Popeye, Betty Boop) and Walter Lantz (Woody Woodpecker), but my two biggest influences were Disney Studios (for their art and storytelling) and Warner Bros. (for their anarchic humor).

Humor in School

I grew up in the rural mill town of Oregon City—not a hotbed of culture, so most of my artistic influences came via magazines and TV. But I was cultured enough to become the so-called class artist, which didn't mean a lot in a school full of blue-collar kids. In fact, many of my teachers made fun of my attempts to draw or tell funny stories.

JUNIOR HIGH DRAWING (AGE 13)

I remember one time in art class when I did a woodcut of a sexy cartoon woman, the teacher hated it and gave me an F because it "wasn't serious art." Another teacher, in sixth grade, showed a humorous story I wrote to the entire class as an example of what *not* to write.

It was okay for me to draw cartoons in the school newspaper, but God forbid I should do that during class. I think my teachers were afraid of losing control over the class; their fear of any semblance of anarchy made them come down hard on cartoons and nip the practice in the bud.

Fortunately, I had my dad to look up to, which kept my faith in the power of humor.

I have a very strong memory of an animated short film I saw at the Portland State film screenings. It was called "The Do-It-Yourself Cartoon Kit," by Bob Godfrey. He was a big influence on Monty Python and Terry Gilliam in particular. But what really impressed me was that this film was not made in Hollywood; it was something called an "independent short." Wow, you mean you don't have to work for the big studios? Someone can make a film by themselves? What a concept!

Oregon's Climate

Another powerful influence on my childhood was the natural climate of Oregon's Willamette Valley.

Winners are:
Terry Schandel
Bill Plympton
Margaret Lambert
Lauren Swick

ME, SECOND FROM LEFT, JUNIOR HIGH SCHOOL POSTER CONTEST (1959)

In terms of rainfall, it wasn't the highest—in fact, we rarely got big rainstorms like the East Coast does—but what we did get was a constant drizzle, day after day, week after week, month after month. It was kind of like those Chinese water tortures—drip, drip, drip on the forehead. Some people say that Oregon's climate contributes to the highest rates of alcoholism and suicides in the country; I don't know if that's true, but I wouldn't be surprised if it were.

However, such weather also forces people to find indoor activities, such as drawing. In fact, there many great cartoonists and animators who hail from the Portland area: Will Vinton, Matt Groening, Brad Bird, John Callahan, Mike Allred, and Basil Wolverton, plus many others. Also there are a lot of psychos from the area—Gary Gilmore, Ted Bundy, and Tonya Harding—so those are your career choices, cartoonist or psycho. I get the best of both worlds: I put psychos in my cartoons.

The constant rain also creates a magical, mystical feeling of nature that is very strong in the Northwest. Walking through the woods, one becomes aware of a mist from low-lying clouds, or a giant fog bank rolling through, and the world becomes very blurry. One sees strange shapes in the distance—is that a man or a monster? A bigfoot? A Loch Ness monster? Or perhaps Tonya Harding?

The imagination is sparked by the fantastic natural phenomena that occur every day in Oregon. Everything is magical; nothing seems real. My brain was caught up in this wonderful fantasy environment.

SCHOOL CARTOON (AGE 13)

SCHOOL CARTOON (AGE 14)

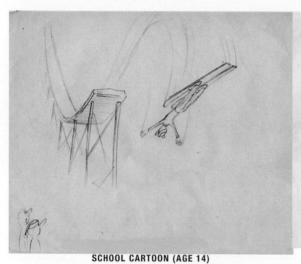

SCHOOL CARTOON (AGE 14)

Caption: "YET, HE CERTAINLY HAS FINE FORM!"

CARTOON FOR SCHOOL PAPER (AGE 14)

WATERCOLOR (AGE 15)

SCHOOL CARTOON (AGE 12)

CLASSMATE (AGE 17)

RAPIDOGRAPH (AGE 21)

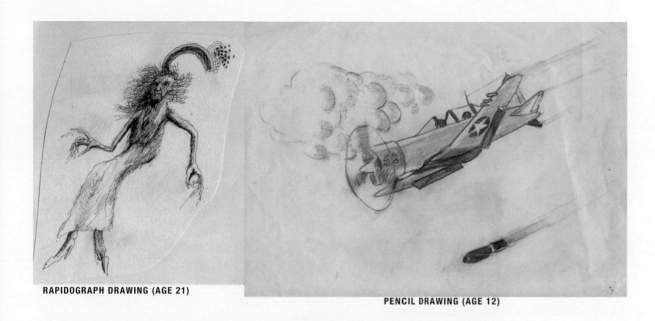

RAPIDOGRAPH DRAWING (AGE 21)

PENCIL DRAWING (AGE 12)

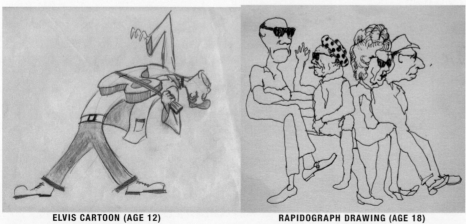

ELVIS CARTOON (AGE 12)   RAPIDOGRAPH DRAWING (AGE 18)

The Big Apple

In 1969, I moved to New York City to attend art school at the School of Visual Arts.

Because the animation industry was pretty much in a coma at the time, you can imagine the kind of animation teachers I got back then. One assignment was to make a film using "purple" as the central concept. That was it—that was all the instruction I got. I needed technical knowledge: how to make timing sheets, how to use a field guide, how to use the camera, and how to create sound and music tracks. So much to learn, and all this guy did to inspire me was to tell me to center my film around "purple"! This was in the hippie 1960s.

I remember another assignment, in which I was supposed to take part in some kind of street theater. "In high school, you follow rules," said the teacher. "In college, you break rules." So I came to class on the subway one day wearing reading glasses—but these weren't normal glasses. They had tiny headlights on both sides. I looked like one of those alien mole-people with eyes that glowed in the dark—but blasé New York straphangers all ignored me because they'd seen it all before.

I think that's when I realized that performance art wasn't for me.

CENTRAL PARK SKETCH FOR *NEW YORKER*, 1978 (REJECTED)

The biggest change in moving to New York was being exposed to real culture. At the time, NYC had recently become the center of world culture. All of the famous artists, great orchestras, top music clubs, popular magazines, newspapers, art directors, illustrators, and design studios were based in New York, and I wanted to experience them all.

People like John Cassavetes, R. O. Blechman, Saul Steinberg, Jules Feiffer, David Levine, Tomi Ungerer, Seymour Chwast, Andy Warhol, Robert Rauschenberg, Charles Addams, Ralph Bakshi, Milton Glaser—these were all New Yorkers and people I aspired to be like.

Also, I was finally able to live near a movie theater—and not just one, but hundreds of them, some of which regularly showed art films, indie films, foreign films, and animated films. After growing up in the woods of Oregon, I felt like I had to catch up on 70 years of filmmaking. I wanted to see all of the classic films that I'd heard about, and all of the new hot films coming out, so I'd set aside one day a week to see films, living off popcorn and pop, rushing from one 50¢ cinema to the next, just in time to watch the opening credits.

The Thalia, a wonderful art-house cinema on the Upper West Side, would occasionally screen a monthlong tribute to old cartoons called "Cartoonal Knowledge," curated by the genius collector and animator Greg Ford.

The great thing about that show was that often he'd program films that were totally unavailable on TV, simply because they were too sexy, racist, violent, off-beat, or just too bizarre for the TV stations' narrow guidelines. That's where I really discovered the amazing films of Tex Avery and Bob Clampett, two of my cartoon heroes. Even today, you can see the influence of those two men on my films.

Their work showed me that it's really important to try different ideas in animation and to get experimental and try to push the limits of people's expectations and sensibilities—that's where the best humor lives. But I will talk more about that in later chapters.

I set a schedule for my rise to fame and fortune:

- In my twenties, my plan was to build up my cartoonal knowledge and see every film ever made.
- I figured that in my thirties, I'd develop a killer style that would catapult me to success.

- In my forties, I'd become a household name and get very famous.
- In my fifties, I'd cash in on my famous name and style and become fabulously wealthy.
- Then, in my sixties, I could mellow out by a fabulous beach mansion in the Hamptons and take whatever job appealed to me.

Well, that's not exactly how it played out—I did develop a style that is uniquely my own and is easily identifiable. However, my other goals fell flat. I'm in my mid-sixties now, still trying to cash in on my talent, and it's just not happening. The Hamptons beach mansion is a faraway fantasy—basically, I'm barely making it from month to month, just paying my bills, but making the films I want to make.

So why have I never broken into the "big time"? How come I can't cash in on my unique style and talents? I'll get to that later on in the book.

Print Cartoons

As you read in an earlier chapter, the 1970s were a desert as far as great animation was concerned. So as soon as I left art school, I began taking my portfolio around looking for illustration work—but what to put in my portfolio? There was no career in animation, so I was back to the dilemma from my childhood days: what kind of cartoon career did I want—gag cartoons, comic strips, underground comics, illustration, caricature, or political cartoons? Because I was totally broke, I tried to do all of them. Fortunately, it was the Golden Age of Illustration, which eventually ended in the 1990s with the advent of computer technology.

I needed money, and I didn't care how I got it. But it was all right, because I didn't really have my own art style—I borrowed a lot from my favorite artists (in fact, I still do), so in those early art days I was looking for both a career and a style.

It wasn't until 1974, when I started my political cartoon strip *Plympton*, that I was forced to clarify my art style. As the schedules for a comic strip are often quite short, I had to draw very fast to make my deadlines, so my drawing style became very loose. Also, I had to come up with a funny idea in a matter of minutes, which trained my brain to

UNPUBLISHED RAPIDOGRAPH ILLUSTRATION, 1978

MY POLITICAL CARTOON STRIP, 1986

always be thinking of jokes, and to turn an idea into humor—to find the funniest way to tell a story.

I think those two talents that I developed are very important to the success I have today, such as it is.

"Your Face"

By the mid 1980s, animation was starting to come back. Also, filmmakers such as Spike Lee and Jim Jarmusch were showing how directors could make their own films without the money or prestige of the Hollywood system. In fact, their movies were better *because* of the lack of Hollywood's involvement.

I figured, "Damn, I better make my films now, or it'll be too late!" I thought that if I waited, I'd be too old to make my childhood dream of being an animator come true.

With very little knowledge of how to make a film, I started making drawings of a man's face that would transform into bizarre and humorous shapes. And I hired my friend, musical genius Maureen McElheron, to create a song that this head-warping guy could sing—and voilà, she wrote "Your Face."

Originally, I'd thought of this film as an experiment—to see if I could actually make a film on my own. I wanted to learn the craft, and what better way was there than to just start experimenting?

I remember the first time I showed the film; it was at an ASIFA competition screening in New York in 1986. (I'll explain ASIFA in a later chapter.) The theater was filled with NYC professionals like R. O. Blechman, George Griffin, Howard Beckerman, and Michael Sporn. I was in the back of the room because I was so embarrassed by my unprofessional, goofball film. But about five seconds in, people started to laugh! I was amazed! My whole body started to glow and shake—this was the laughter I'd never gotten from all of my print cartoons. It was like a drug—I was on a no-chemical high. I needed more; I was hooked!

Afterward, everyone came over to me and asked if I was Bill Plympton. They asked me out for drinks, and I felt like I was home. The next day, I called all of my magazine and newspaper clients and told them I was quitting print. They all thought I was crazy and said things like, "Don't you know animation is dead?" But I said that I thought I could make a living doing animation.

That goofy little film, "Your Face," went on to get an Oscar nomination and became a big hit all over the world. I took it to Annecy, the great French animation festival—and after the screening there, many people approached me and offered all kinds of money for the TV and theatrical rights in their respective countries.

"Wa-hoo!" I said to myself. "I'm actually making money on my film! I think I'll have to make more!" And in quick order, I churned out a string of short animated films that were all big hits: "How to Kiss," "One of Those Days," "25 Ways to Quit Smoking," and "Plymptoons." I was on my way!

In the mid 1980s, there were three major outlets for animated shorts. The MTV animation department was headed by Abby Terkuhle, who became a big supporter of weird, wild, and funny animation on the channel. He discovered my film "Your

Face" at Annecy, and for about ten years, I was the Animation Golden Boy on MTV. My shorts were on *Liquid Television* (and later *Cartoon Sushi*), plus I made station IDs for them, promos for the MTV Movie Awards, and a lot of other interstitials. Even today, as I make appearances all over the world, people still remember me as "that MTV animator guy" or "the colored pencil guy."

Concurrently, there were two very popular theatrical compilation shows touring the United States. The Tournée of Animation, organized by Terry Thoren and Ron Diamond, was the more professional of the two, and I was very honored to have my work included with the best animated shorts from around the world. This traveling show represented the high road to animation distribution.

Taking the low road was Spike & Mike's Animation Show, which later evolved into Spike & Mike's Sick and Twisted Show, founded by Spike Decker and (the now-late) Mike Gribble. Their screenings were much more raucous—in fact, it was the closest thing to a cartoon circus.

They wore weird costumes, the audience bounced giant beach balls around, and of course there was Scotty, the Magic Dog. I'd often attend and share the stage with Weird Al Yankovic, John Lasseter, Marv Newland, and of course the crazy Mike Gribble. Those were heady days for animated short filmmakers!

"YOUR FACE," COLORED PENCIL, 1986

Chapter 3

MAKING AN ANIMATED FILM

CARTOON BY CORDELL BARKER

Now I'm going to tell you how you can be a success like Bill Plympton.

There are certainly many ways to be successful in the animation business, and mine isn't the only way, but I believe that a lot of my ideas are not only helpful but hopefully also inspirational, and that they can help you on the way to a big career in cartoons.

What I want to do is show you my procedure for making a film. It's basically the same for a short as it is for a feature. I see three major steps in filmmaking: raising the money, making the film, and selling the film.

The middle one is the easiest and the most fun— that's the glamorous part. It's the step that everyone considers first. However, the first and third parts are more difficult, but just as important and these are the areas where most filmmakers fail. So pay attention; we'll start at the beginning.

MY ONE GIG AS A GAP MODEL, 1995. PHOTO BY GUS VAN SANT.

Raising the Money

Raising money is the most difficult hurdle in making a film—in fact, for many filmmakers, it's a brick wall. What's that phrase? GTFM: Get The Friggin' Money (or something like that). That's the kind of attitude you have to have. This is where 80 percent of film projects fail. Before you go out look ing for hard-to-find money, you need six things:

1. A great idea

2. A synopsis

3. A budget

4. A marketing plan

5. Concept art

6. A title

Idea

You can't have a great film without an idea or a concept—but where can you find a great idea? Look no further, animation students, because in this section, I'll tell you my Eight Easy Ways to Find an Idea for Your Film.

A great work of art always feels like it magically appeared from the Hand of God—but that's the trick, to make it seem like it just effortlessly flowed from my brain into the screen when in fact I labored long and hard to make it feel so natural and easy.

People say that all you need is a great idea, and the film makes itself; I disagree. Even though I may have what I think is a great idea, there's a long way to go before I have a great film. In the rest of this book, I'll discuss the procedure for completing a film, but for now let's talk about those eight ways to get great, or even good, ideas:

1. Carry an idea notepad with you at all times. If you have a drawing pad, even better.

2. Get outside, preferably in a crowded city. I live in New York, which is a cartoon city. I can walk one block through its crowded streets and get three or four great ideas for films. You can also visit other cultures in other countries for a fresh perspective on your own traditions and lifestyles. When you travel to foreign countries, the surrealism of the United States becomes apparent.

3. Be receptive; keep your brain open for any idea, whether you're watching TV, reading a newspaper, or talking to a friend. If something strikes you as strange or funny, there's usually a good idea there. And often you have to play with it, bend it, or bounce it around your brain before it becomes something that has great possibilities. But the brain should always be like a vacuum cleaner, or a dry sponge, sucking up ideas constantly and then analyzing the possibilities of a great story or funny gag.

4. Daydream. In grade school, I was always looking out the window and daydreaming, and it drove my teachers mad. They always disciplined me for being inattentive—but now I often spend an hour just laying in bed, letting my mind wander anywhere it wants to go, and I find lots of ideas there. The more you visit the fantasyland inside your brain, the more creative you become. Exercise your imagination muscles.

5. Be curious about life. Why do certain phenomena happen the way they do? You must have the curiosity of a child.

My film "Guard Dog" was inspired by me questioning an incident I witnessed in a local park. A dog on a leash was barking at a squirrel, and I wondered, "Why is this dog threatened by a harmless, fearful squirrel?" And when I went inside the dog's brain and saw things from his point of view, I realized that he felt afraid that the squirrel would attack his master and he'd lose his meal ticket. Well, that crazy scenario inspired the short film and led to my most successful character and many sequels.

Other mysteries of life: Why do birds fly in flocks? Where does belly-button lint come from?

Why do guys have nipples? I'm sure you can come up with your own mystery of life.

6. Blur your vision. I often find that miscommunication, misunderstanding, and misperception lead to great ideas.

7. I also find a lot of ideas in other people's previous work—books, paintings at a museum, graphic novels, great animation, illustration, plays, and even music. Ah, but you might say, "That's stealing!" No, I don't want you to adapt someone else's story and put your name on it. I'm just thinking that an interesting visual or paragraph has the potential to become its own story. I'm inspired by a lot of art, and again my brain goes off on its own train of thought and falls into the stream of consciousness, which often results in unique and inventive ideas—it's funny how creativity is contagious like that.

8. Look for ideas that have never been expressed before. I have an expression, "Wouldn't it be cool … ." For example, wouldn't it be cool to see what would happen if an asshole guy woke up one morning with angel wings on his back ("Idiots and Angels")? Or, wouldn't it be cool if a guy found out he had god-like powers to change reality ("I Married a Strange Person")? These weird ideas spawned some of my best films.

Synopsis (Storyboard)

The synopsis, or story summary, should be about two pages long and should bring out all of the compelling aspects of the story, whether it's a book you fell in love with, a short story, or an idea you came up with, like a crazy dream you had in the middle of the night.

I rarely use my dreams because they're far too mundane—me doing the laundry, or cleaning the apartment—exciting stuff like that. The only film I've created using a dream was *Hair High*—and that was a doozy of a dream.

You want the synopsis to engage the reader immediately, with some kind of hook—something fresh and different. Don't go into a lot of plot detail, just present a flavor of the humor, characters, drama, romance, or whatever the genre of the story is.

To make the process a lot easier, you might want to create a script or a storyboard. Sometimes the money people will accept a synopsis or an outline, but if you really want to make the deal, it helps to deliver a script or a storyboard.

One of the biggest problems that I have with Hollywood is that these executives are used to reading scripts. They believe that the scripts are like bibles. That's all well and good, but what happens if the film has no dialog? In other words, what's in the script if there is no one talking? It's just descriptions of what you'll be seeing on the screen. I tell them, "I have a storyboard that shows what you'll be seeing on the screen; so I don't have to describe it in words." Then these executives say, "I'm sorry, I only read scripts."

This *bugs the hell* out of me. Films are great when they're "cinematic." What does "cinematic" mean? It means visual storytelling—which is exactly what my storyboards are intended to do!

So this is just a warning: if you're presenting a film to Hollywood, and there's very little or no dialog, you may have to write a script anyway.

Of course, I prefer a storyboard. So much of the film is displayed in the artwork. But hey, maybe that's why I'm still financing my own films.

Budget

The budget should also be very preliminary (one page); mention only a few of the more important categories and no details. The film's budget is based on a number of important factors:

- How long will the film be? A feature film costs somewhere between $200,000 (my kind of budget) and $200 million (a Pixar budget). A short film's budget will be anywhere from $2,000 to $1 million or more.
- Who is the audience? Is it a kid film or an adult film? Will it play in festivals? Theaters? Television, cable, DVD, pay-per-view (PPV), Internet? Is it geared toward males or females? These are very important questions.
- What technique will be used? The cheapest technique (for me, anyway), is drawing by hand. Stop-motion can be inexpensive (depending on the characters), but it has a very long production time,

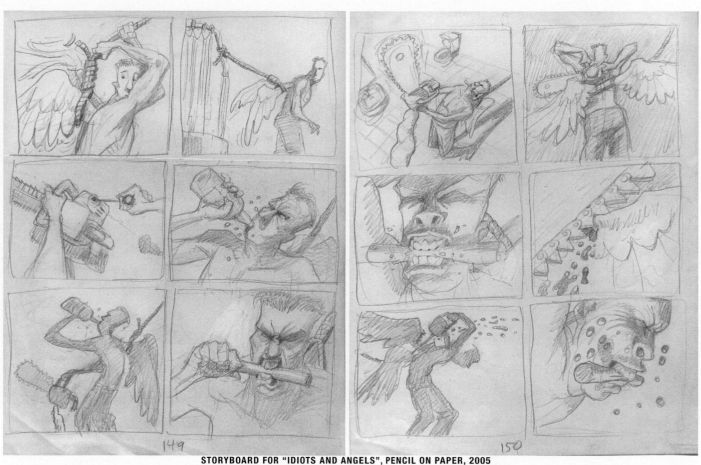

STORYBOARD FOR "IDIOTS AND ANGELS", PENCIL ON PAPER, 2005

which raises the budget. Flash is a very popular method now; it's cheap and fast and can look very good. The most expensive technique is 3D computer graphics—this technique takes forever, with many artists working together, but it looks great if done right. And it's very commercial now.

- What sort of production will it be? Do you foresee hiring a lot of employees? Will it be created in the United States or overseas? Can you work via the Internet? Can you do a lot of the art yourself? Are there any stars or expensive songs in the film? How long will the production take—one year, two years, three years? The longer the production time, the more expensive it will be.

Here is a sample budget for "Idiots and Angels."

Marketing Plan

You next need a marketing plan. Obviously, any investor needs to know how he or she will get their money back. The investors need to show a profit, unless of course they love giving their money away to struggling animators who like making self-indulgent, masturbatory films.

Talk about your past sales to other distribution companies, or, if you don't have past sales, any connections you have with distribution companies. Connections are very important for any kind of business. I can't overstate how important it is to know as many people in the business as possible. It behooves you to be gregarious and friendly.

Another way to make connections is through the festival circuit. Even if you don't have a film screening in the festivals, they're usually great places to hook up with important people in the biz—especially at parties or while waiting in line to go see a film. That's where you meet the movers and shakers—who knows, maybe they're aware of a distributor looking for films.

IDIOTS AND ANGELS BUDGET		MY BUDGET	NORMAL LOW-BUDGET INDIE ANIMATED FEATURE
PRODUCER	Bill Plympton	$0.00 (deferred)	$100,000.00
CO-PRODUCER	Biljana Labovic	$20,000.00	$100,000.00
DIRECTOR	Bill Plympton	$0.00 (deferred)	$100,000.00
WRITER/STORYBOARDS	Bill Plympton	$0.00 (deferred)	$100,000.00
ANIMATOR	Bill Plympton	$0.00 (deferred)	$500,000.00
CLEANING	Various Crew	$10,000.00	$10,000.00
COMPOSITING	Various Crew	$10,000.00	$10,000.00
CAMERA	Kerri Allegretta	$20,000.00	$20,000.00
COLORING	Biljana Labovic	$3,000.00	$3,000.00
EDITING	Kevin Palmer	$20,000.00	$20,000.00
SOUND	Greg Sextro	$12,000.00	$12,000.00
MUSIC	Various Artists	$10,000.00	$10,000.00
DIGITAL TRANSFER	Technicolor	$25,000.00	$25,000.00
PRINTS	Technicolor	$5,000.00	$5,000.00
MISCELLANEOUS		$10,000.00	$10,000.00
OVERHEAD		$50,000.00	$50,000.00
	TOTAL	$195,000.00	$1,075,000.00

Don't be shy, like I usually am—go up and talk to these people, even if you don't have a film to sell yet. Get their business cards, talk about films; then, when you've got a project, it's a lot easier to start contacting people and get your foot in the door.

In your marketing plan, also talk about theatrical sales, nontheatrical sales, TV, DVD, Internet and ancillary sales. Talk about the target audience; tell them how popular animation is. Everyone loves animation, and everyone wants animation.

Animation is "evergreen"—because it's art, it can be timeless. A film like *Snow White and the Seven Dwarfs* was released 80 years ago but makes more money now than when it was first released. People should be aware of the higher intrinsic value of cartoons over live-action.

If you're going to sell your film, it's very important to define your audience. In fact, that's one of the first questions distributors ask me: "Who is the audience?"

In the past, my audience has been mostly males aged 16–30, but recently, with the completion of three films—"The Fan and the Flower," "The Cow Who Wanted to Be a Hamburger," and "Idiots and Angels"—I've expanded my audience to include more women, older fans, and kids. I don't know if this trend will continue, because I'll always enjoy making films that are a bit transgressive and politically incorrect.

There's no way I can compete with Pixar and DreamWorks for the family film audience. I don't have the money or the talent, so I'm happy making films for an older, hipper audience. I sort of consider myself the Tarantino of animation, and I like that. But if I were starting out today and looking for work in the film business, I'd definitely start at the big, family-oriented studios.

I don't like to narrow my audience, I pray for universal appeal. I hate snobbish, purist filmmakers—people who eschew wacky gags and prurient violence. They take their films way too seriously; they want their film to elevate the soul. Come on, get real! That shows a certain disdain for the common audience.

I'll tell you a story. I was working at a grocery store when I was around 18, and my boss had a grandson he was very proud of. Knowing I was a painter, he asked me to do a portrait of the kid. I agreed, took a snapshot of him, and did a cute oil painting of the 4-year-old boy.

Then, I began to study art at Portland State, where the teachers infused me with ideas of cubism, collage, abstract painting, conceptual art, and so many other new ideas that make up modern art, and I felt that if I was going to be a great artist, I had to learn these new styles of painting.

Not wanting to be old-fashioned, I changed my whole style to incorporate a lot more experimentation, and as I progressed along this road to the avant-garde, I felt bad about the painting I'd done for my grocery store boss, so I asked him if I could get the portrait back and touch it up a bit to make it much more professional. He reluctantly returned the oil painting to me, and I set about reshaping the painting so that posterity and the critics would herald me as the new Picasso.

Of course, when I showed the painting to my boss, he was stunned, and a few weeks later he got the courage to tell me he much preferred the earlier version. In fact, they were now afraid to show the painting, and it probably got displayed facing a wall in their attic. This was a very important lesson for me: know your audience!

I talk to a lot of young filmmakers about their new projects, and when I tell them their idea is very noncommercial and will be very hard to sell, invariably they'll say that they don't care, that it's a project they're compelled to make! But what about the audience? They might say it doesn't matter, that they're making the film for themselves. I then ask them, "Then why bother showing the film to an audience?"

I consider myself a populist—I love Frank Capra films, and I unashamedly love *Titanic* and *Avatar*. So many people are afraid to say they like something that's popular—they don't want to appear to be undiscriminating. I'm very democratic. I believe that the public is the true decider of what's great and what's not. What's that old saying about a fork in the road, and taking the path that's less traveled? Well, I tend to like the one that's more traveled because you meet so many more interesting people on it. But, as I travel down that popular path, I like to walk it in my own unique way.

Concept Art

Concept art is a very important part of selling the film. You should present a sample of the finished film, either as a piece of concept art or as a short, inexpensive pilot or demo. If you are unable to create the sample yourself, try to find someone such as a professional illustrator or an art student (depending on your finances) to create some artwork for you. Obviously, if you can show a pilot—some sample animation and story—it makes your film a lot easier to sell.

I like to create the pilot as a short film; that way, I'm able to enter it into festivals and perhaps win some prizes—who knows, maybe even an Oscar nomination—and then it's a piece of cake to make sales or get investors. If you can't afford to make the pilot, be sure that the concept art shows off the main characters and is representative of the style and story that you want to make. Remember, a quality presentation is very important because it reflects the quality of the finished film.

CONCEPT ART FOR *HAIR HIGH*, PAINTED CEL, 2003

CONCEPT ART FOR *CHEATIN'*, PENCIL ON PAPER, 2008

Title

A final important ingredient in making a compelling pitch is a catchy, intriguing title. I prefer to use one- or two-word titles, like "Draw!" "Your Face," *Hair High*, "Guard Dog," and so on because I think they're easier to remember. I've used a few long titles, like "I Married a Strange Person" and "The Cow Who Wanted to Be a Hamburger," but often those were take-offs of existing titles, like *I Married a Witch* or *The Man Who Would Be King*.

A big waste of money is the so-called title search. Often producers or investors will ask you to get a title search to make sure that your title is unique, which often costs around $500. Why one must get a title search is beyond me—a title cannot be copyrighted, and there are numerous films out there that have the same titles, and no one has complained. For example, there were two big films called *The Illusionist*, one live action and one animated. It didn't cause any scandals or lawsuits. I just tell my investors that I looked up the prospective title in Leonard Maltin's *Film Guide* and found no duplicate or similar name.

So now that you have your pitching package, you're ready to raise your money.

If you bought this book hoping to learn everything about financing your film, then I hate to break the sad news to you—this is the wrong book for you. But I will give you some alternatives to self-financing.

Grants

I don't use grant money. I find that it's a lot of work filling out the application paperwork, jumping through hoops, and often changing the project to fit certain standards, which I think can really dilute the purity of the original concept. Also, there's often a long delay before you get the notice of the awarding of the grant, and then another delay before you actually get the money.

Family and Friends

Family and friends are a much-used source of financing. I know a lot of filmmakers who have used a trust fund (or a rich relative) to make their films. The problem is that this kind of money is so easy to get that these filmmakers tend to have less regard for the audience—the film becomes more of a vanity project. They don't need to make the money back, so what the hell—they just make the film for themselves. I see a lot of these films in festivals, and they win a lot of awards because they're challenging and avant-garde, but they don't speak to the audience and rarely get distributed.

Hollywood

I don't consider myself an expert on soliciting funding from Hollywood studios, or any kind of studio, for that matter. I do remember that back in 1988 I was contacted by the William Morris Agency to become a client because I'd been nominated for an Oscar for "Your Face." They thought I'd be the next Matt Groening, so they brought me out to Los Angeles (actually, I paid) for a week of meetings with production companies to try and sell a TV show.

I got the usual "You're a genius!" "We're dying to work with you!" "Let's make a deal!" and "We love your work!" … blah blah blah, only to return to New York and find out that nothing happened except that I wasted a week's time when I could have been making a new film.

Now, maybe I'm just a bad salesman, and I don't know how to speak their language. Pitching is a very special talent: one has to be supremely self-confident or be a great actor. I'm neither—I always have doubts about the popularity of any of my films. I like the ideas, but often my concepts are so strange that I think that the audience will hate them.

Also, I'm not a good liar—I can't pretend that this film is going to change the course of Western civilization. In the back of my brain, I have a constant fear that no one will like or laugh at my film, and consequently, as I'm pitching an idea, if I see any sign of boredom or annoyance in my audience, my enthusiasm is crushed. I lose confidence and I start agreeing with the decision makers that my film project is a turkey and asking why I'm wasting everyone's time.

But I probably have the wrong attitude. You must believe that your project is going to make a billion dollars, that it will be the next *Avatar*, win an armload of Oscars, and then convince the producers of its greatness! I've heard of some animators who dress up in wild animal costumes and put on amateur theatrical productions with music from a boombox and maybe even bring in some celebrities to help get the buyers excited. I'm sure *that* will stick in the brain of an executive producer when he or she decides which projects to greenlight.

In my career, I've never found so many wankers as I have in Hollywood. I've tried to determine why, and I think I've come up with an answer: the glamour and prestige of Hollywood (such as it is) draws people from all over the world to become these "players"—whether they have talent or not (usually not). But to become players, they'll say anything to anybody, because they've become actors themselves, in the pretend world of movie production—they don't care if they lie, because they've sold their souls to the dream of one day actually being a real moviemaker.

Kickstarter and Internet

There are other ways I can raise money, of course: I can hold a benefit screening and show the work in progress, also auctioning off original artwork (I've done that a number of times). Maybe I could hold a $100-per-person intimate dinner with Bill Plympton, with everyone receiving a free caricature.

A couple of times I've opened up my studio to outsiders for an art sale, sort of like an animation-themed garage sale. Hell, I have about 100,000 pieces of original art from my films, just sitting around.

Or you can try the Internet, sites like Kickstarter. Over the past two years, I've been resurrecting Winsor McCay's last animated short, "The Flying House." And it's been a very labor-intensive chore because each frame has to be cleaned and colored individually. Plus, I have to put in sound effects, music, and voices.

The finished film will make very little money (I didn't do it for the money), and I've had a lot of out-of-pocket expenses on the project, so I decided to go the Kickstarter route.

My good friend and fund-raising genius Signe Baumane warned me against it, though. She said it would be too much work, and there was the possibility that I might not reach my goal and therefore have to forfeit all of the pledged money.

But Matthew Modine and his producer, Adam Rackoff, encouraged me to do it. They said they would make the documentary pitch for my project and handle the day-to-day duties for a small service fee. So I said, "Let's do it!" and we began our Kickstarter campaign. It worked fairly easily.

It helped that we had Matthew Modine, Patricia Clarkson (who provided voices), and Winsor McCay's name to drop in the campaign. We also mentioned the antagonism that our project was instigating. Because we were colorizing an animation master's piece of work, we got a shitstorm of angry protests from film scholars and archivists, and we used that controversy to get publicity and more sympathy from potential donors.

We set our goal at $10,000, and we reached that in just two weeks. Ultimately, we closed out at just under $20,000. Of course, we still had to send gifts to the backers, and Matthew and Adam got their cut as producers, but I still made enough to finish off "The Flying House."

So I recommend Kickstarter or any other Internet funding site. They seem to be the wave of the future for financing films, and it's also a great way to raise awareness for a project.

SCENE FROM WINSOR MCCAY AND BILL PLYMPTON'S FILM "THE FLYING HOUSE", 1921/2011

Self-Investment

Self-investment works best for me. People say that investing your money in your own film is sort of like a lawyer defending himself in court—he has a fool for a client.

I disagree; if I've worked on a film for years I know the story and style better than anyone else, so I'm the best person to put money into the project. If I don't believe in my film and myself, why should someone else?

Sure, it's a gamble—but I don't play the lottery, horses, or the slots in Vegas. I believe that the payoff for my film has a much better chance than any of those. In fact, so far I've been a winner. Most all of my shorts and half of my features have been profitable, so I've been on a winning streak. Why give my winnings to some big fat-cat who had nothing to do with the creative side of filmmaking?

But here are some of the downsides to self-investment:

1. You need money to start (not a lot, if you follow my Dogma, described in the following section).

2. You won't have a large publicity machine for support, unless you can also entice a big distributor to get involved.

3. People might think that it must be a stupid project because you couldn't entice a Hollywood studio to back you.

4. It will be more difficult to get distribution.

Yet the pros, for me, outweigh the cons:

1. I always have final cut on the project.

2. I finish the project on my own schedule.

3. There are no boring meetings with executives meddling with the story or characters.

4. There are no marketing people worrying about the merchandising possibilities, or the ratings, or the audience.

5. I can do whatever the hell I want!

6. When the theaters pay, none of the money goes to distributors, agents, lawyers, financers, or other producers—it all comes to me! Yeah!

Plympton's Dogma

It's hard to decide where to place my famous Plympton Dogma within this book. But somehow it seems appropriate to put it here in the beginning, near the financing information, because my dogma is essentially about the business of films, not the creative side. So here are my three Golden Rules for success in short films (and features, too).

Dogma Point #1: Make Your Film *Short*

Whether it's a short or a feature, it shouldn't run too long. I judge a lot of film festivals, and if I see a short film with a running time of 20 minutes, already I hate that film. I don't want to see that film. Why? Because if it's a bad film, then I'm stuck watching 20 minutes of crap! But if it's only 5 minutes of crap, that's okay. I can let my mind wander for 5 minutes, then be ready for the next great film.

Also, it's very difficult to sell a 20-minute film. Cinemas won't want it (because it would take time away from showing a feature). DVD collections won't want it. TV stations don't want to buy and show a 20-minute film, and the Internet prefers films in the 2- to 5-minute range. Plus, it's a lot cheaper to make a 5-minute film.

Dogma Point #2: Make Your Film *Cheap*!

I run an independent film studio. I have to pay my employees, overhead, and make a living, and like I said earlier, I don't take grants, corporate, or Hollywood money. So it's very important that my films are successful and make a profit. If I spent $50,000 or even $1 million (like some shorts cost these days), I'd have a very beautiful film, but I'd be out of business in a week. The cost of my films runs about $1,000 per minute. If I can keep my film budgets in that vicinity, I'll always be able to show a profit.

There are a number of ways to keep the budget low:

- Don't use expensive voice-over talent.
- Don't use expensive music by famous artists.
- Don't use very slow, work-intensive computer programs, such as Maya.

- Don't have a long production time.
- Don't use a large number of people in the production.

Dogma Point #3: Make the Film *Funny*

I don't know why this point is true, but it's a lot easier to sell a funny film than a serious film.

If you want to make a film about your inner turmoil, an abstract film, or a film about politics, go ahead, but no one is going to want to watch it, except for your parents. And no one will buy it.

Everyone loves stories, from kids' bedtime stories to thousand-page novels. I see so many films that are avant-garde and abstract; while watching them, I spend my time searching for any kind of plot or meaning. It's simple; it's human nature to look for reflections of oneself in life's many experiences, and that goes for films, no matter how obtuse. And if you can also tell a story in a funny way, people like it even more.

To demonstrate the difference, I remember when I was nominated for an Oscar in 2005; my film "Guard Dog" was up against a Canadian film called "Ryan," a computer-animated film created by an artistic genius named Chris Landreth. His film broke all my Dogma rules. It was long—about 16 minutes. It was expensive—it probably cost around a million dollars. And it wasn't particularly funny—it was the tragic story of a drug-addicted alcoholic Canadian animator.

But you know what? "Ryan" won the Oscar—and it deserved to win. It was a much better film than mine. It's a masterpiece, but it will never show a profit, because it was such an expensive film to produce. But that's okay, because it was a Canadian film, and the Canadians prefer prizes over profits. They make films to glorify Canadian culture, and that's great!

But I can't do that—I need to make money. I need to pay for my staff and my studio. So when I make a film that wins awards but loses money, it's a disaster. It's interesting; I look at my Dogma points—short, cheap, and funny—and it describes all of my girlfriends (yes, that's a bad joke).

"BAMBI MEETS GODZILLA", MARV NEWLAND, 1972

Another wonderful example I like to talk about is a film called "Bambi Meets Godzilla," by the great Marv Newland. It follows all of my Dogma points perfectly. It's very short—about a minute and a half. It's cheap—I heard he spent $500 making the film. There are only about 15 drawings in the whole film—and it's terrifically funny.

That film has gone on to be a huge success. I heard that it's made over $100,000 over the years. It's the *Deep Throat* of animation. God, I wish I could make a film as good as "Bambi Meets Godzilla." That's my career goal: to make a film that's more successful than Marv Newland's famous short. But I fear I never will: there's only one Marv Newland.

Alternative Funding

I'm now going to suggest some more very creative ways to raise capital. It's often the inventive and unorthodox ideas that bring in the big bucks.

There's lots of grant money out there for new and revolutionary techniques in marketing and animation. See the table on the next page for a few that have never been tried.

TECHNIQUE	POSSIBLE REVENUE
Finger on frosted-window animation	$10,000 in grant money
Making a film using the side edges of the paper (in these days of low carbon-imprint, this might be a good way to also get some EPA money)	$15,000 in grant money
Toilet paper animation	$10,000 in grant money
If the film is a bomb, you can sell off your drawings as a double-use collectible—bathroom tissue *and* frameable art	$33,000 in artwork sales
Other Funding Ideas: Kidnap your worst film-critic nemesis, and hold him for ransom (remember, any publicity is good publicity in the film business)	$33.42 in ransom money (tops)
Product Promotion Stunts: Organize daredevil stunts to bring in the deep-pocket corporate sponsors, like make a film while going over a waterfall	$40,000 sponsorship

Exploit the rich auto industry	$60,000 sponsorship
Exploit a struggling wildlife park looking for publicity	$20,000 sponsorship
The most dangerous stunt of all—a busy city sidewalk: play Tom Sawyer and invite passersby to draw one frame each, for $10 a piece	$120
Charge $100 for a nude drawing	$4,500,000
Giving your film a grand total of	$4,688,153.42

And you're on your way to making a great film!

Chapter 4

PRODUCTION

Okay, this is the fun part. You've raised your money, and it matches the budget (hopefully). Let's make this sucker!

When I start off on the production of a new feature film, I realize that ahead of me lie two years of solid work, late hours, and the spending of a lot of money. But I never really consider that a problem because the idea for the new film is so strong and so clever that it will revolutionize our present understanding of animation. I see myself getting the Oscar handed to me by John Lasseter, who says to me, "Bill, you're going to change the world with this film! You're going to win the prestigious Nobel Peace Prize, because it's genius!"

And that's how you have to think about your project, because how else are you going to get through the long, difficult process of making a film?

Creating a Studio

The next step is to hire a staff. Build a team. I get a lot of my artists from recommendations, which is very important, because I have hired a few people without referrals, and they were disasters. I usually like to give people a one-month trial to see how they work, how fast they are, and how diligent they are.

Good employees are:

1. Punctual

2. Hard-working

3. Fast

4. Efficient

5. Proficient in all the programs (Adobe Photoshop, Adobe Flash, Apple Final Cut Pro)

6. Willing to do anything to help the film

7. Artistic

8. Anxious to learn

9. Pleasant to work with

Bad employees are:

1. Loud and constantly talking

2. Always on the phone

3. Always out to lunch

4. Afraid to try something new and different

5. Smokers

6. Not committed to animation

My own studio is quite small compared to a Hollywood studio. It's a "boutique" studio in the heart of Chelsea in New York City. It's about 1,000 square feet, with a lot of shelves and a few computers.

The shelves are for numerous things—equipment, 35 mm film prints, merchandise (my DVDs, books, posters, and promo items). We have about five computer stations and four employees. John is my office manager; he makes sure that the book-keeping is accurate and that film prints and tapes reach their destinations on time. Lindsay is my art director; she does coloring, typing, and production work. Desirée is my associate producer; she makes sure that all the productions meet their deadlines and handles all of my website and Internet needs. Then we usually have one or two interns, students who come in once a week as part of their classwork.

My general workload is this: I try to create a feature film every two or three years (over the past twenty-five years, I've made ten feature films), and I like to make a new short film once a year—they're so much fun to make. I spice up my routine with the occasional commissioned job, such as a commercial, music video, documentary supplement or feature insert, and I leave lots of time to travel for festivals and speaking engagements.

It's very important for me to have my staff complete the technical side, at which I'm so deficient. The bigger the project, the more I rely on my staff.

A lot of big studios delegate the work to hundreds of artists. The great Matt Groening has very little involvement with *The Simpsons* any more—he'll occasionally go to script readings or approve merchandise and, of course, cash his huge checks. I, on the other hand, create the artwork and monitor production every step of the way to make sure it matches my original concept. And, of course, the checks I cash are much smaller than Matt's.

But I prefer the smaller studio; I like being involved in all aspects of the production. It's not that I'm a megalomaniac; it's just fun to see the film go from concept to pencil test to finished film. It's a real feeling of accomplishment.

I'm a rare exception in the animation business, in that I draw every drawing in all of my films. For me, it's fun, but I don't recommend it for other artists, especially for TV animation, with its quick turnaround time. Delegating parts of the workload is the norm for most animation production, whether it's for TV, film, or commercials.

PLYMPTOONS STUDIO (PHOTO BY SANDRINE FLAMENT)

Chapter 5
STORYTELLING

"Show it, don't say it."

—CLINT EASTWOOD

The Myth of Story

I've been accused of making strange films with weak stories. The critics sometimes say that my stories ramble, and have no focus—that they have too many diversions. There may be some truth to their criticisms, but for me, story isn't the end-all and be-all in the success of a film.

How many times have you heard the expression "all great films start with a great story"? Talk about clichés! Well, I'm sick and tired of hearing that bull. Sure, there are wonderful films that are great because of the story, but please, give me a break! First of all, people describe great film as "cinematic." What does it mean? It means it's a visual experience, something that has nothing to do with words. In fact, I love many films that have either no words or very minimal script—for example, Jacques Tati films,

"The Triplets of Belleville," Georges Méliès, Josef von Sternberg, Terry Gilliam, Tim Burton, Charlie Chaplin, Buster Keaton, and Busby Berkeley. And the films of the Marx Brothers or W. C. Fields, for example, are essentially plotless; they are cavalcades of gag sequences strung together by a weak plot. Or take John Cassavetes, whose films were essentially improvised in front of the camera.

And what the hell was the story for such classics as *2001: A Space Odyssey* or Miyazaki's *Princess Mononoke* or *Howl's Moving Castle*? Did you understand anything in these films? Some other great films that have no real story: *Citizen Kane* (very cinematic) or *Woodstock*. *Yellow Submarine*, the animated classic, was begun without a script.

I could go on and on, but why beat a dead script? If I hear someone use the expression "story is everything" one more time, I'll stick his or her tongue in my electric pencil sharpener—now that's cinematic!

Having said that, I'm trying with each film to get a better, more emotional story. I believe that *Idiots and Angels* came close to achieving a very strong story—and certainly in all of my future films, I want to have the most powerful stories possible.

Intuition

Many of my decisions are made by intuition. Intuition is a very important talent to bring to filmmaking, and I consider it a result of watching a lot of films and being aware of how the audience reacts. Over the years, this experience has become second nature, and it helps me construct my stories.

When I was younger, I'd watch up to eight films in a day—and that's not counting shorts. I did that for two reasons: first, I'd decided that if I really wanted to be a filmmaker, I'd have to study all of the films, present and past, to see what's possible and what's impossible and what works and what doesn't work. Second, I just plain love to watch movies, good and bad. In fact, I would sit in the front row of the theater so that I could be enveloped into the film. I became part of the luminous screen.

I bring this up because once you've made a film, you have to use a lot of self-criticism throughout the process—especially in the story writing phase. And even though it's impossible to remember every scene of every film I've seen, I believe that the stored information gives me a strong intuitive sense of what works and what doesn't. After watching so many films in the big multiplexes, I can almost know when a joke is going to make people laugh and when it isn't.

So that's why I recommend that young filmmakers see as many films as possible. The films that are special and particularly powerful should be seen numerous times and studied and analyzed as to why they work and how they can apply those lessons in the making of their own films.

It's my feeling that a story's flow should resemble a great piece of music or perhaps the sex act. Initially, it's important to attract the attention of the audience, or the "lover." So I prefer to open a film with something very intriguing or dramatic, just to make sure that the audience is involved. This is the flirtation stage.

Then, as in the act of lovemaking, I like to have short but powerful buildups that end in small climaxes, sort of like acts or sequences, but I follow each scene with an even more intense sequence that ratchets up the emotional involvement—so the excitement builds and builds until the final act, which ends in an explosion of sound, fury, sexual fulfillment, and emotional climax. Not all of my films follow this formula, but I try to keep to it as much as possible.

Another key ingredient in a successful story is having a unique idea. As the Monty Python tagline used to say, "And now for something completely different."

My films are often not very successful, perhaps because they are too strange or off-beat. But I'd rather see a different kind of film done badly than a clichéd film done very well. If I have a failure, I want it to be a glorious failure.

I look for the off-beat. It's like when I'm walking down the street. I don't look at all the normal people; my eye is attracted to people who are strange, bizarre, or out of the ordinary—and it's the same way with films. I'm on this earth for a short time; I don't want to create films that conform to the status quo. I want to make art that insults the status quo, that makes people think differently. If I'm in an elevator and everyone has their arms crossed, then I feel compelled to uncross my arms.

A lot of critics call me politically incorrect—well, that's the way I've been since my college days, and it's too late for me to change now. I'll never get rich, but at least I'll have a lot of fun making my films.

"As a producer, be a rational adult. As a director, be a crazy spoiled child."

—BILL PLYMPTON

Conflict

Another very important ingredient in a film's story is conflict. A number of years ago, when Dustin Hoffman won an Academy Award (I believe it was for *Kramer vs. Kramer*), during his acceptance speech, he went on a rant about how impossible it was to give awards to actors. I'm paraphrasing here, but it was something like, "This actor is not better than that actor. And that performance is not better than so and so's performance. It's absurd to give only one award; all the actors should get an Oscar."

Well, it was certainly a well-meant and very democratic outburst, but I believe Dustin missed the whole point of the Oscars. Who the hell's going to watch the Academy Awards if everyone gets a damn prize? No one! That's like the Special Olympics for the handicapped, where everyone gets a prize—and who watches that? People watch only because there's a winner and a loser. Lots of losers, and that's good for ratings. That gives the awards a conflict. It's a contest, like a sporting event. What's more exciting to watch, a baseball game that ends with a score of 20–0, or one that's 21–20?

People are attracted to conflict. And the more competitive the conflict, the more exciting it is. I like to build up all levels of a film's conflicts, so that they culminate or resolve themselves in the last five minutes of the film.

When I was making "The Cow Who Wanted to Be a Hamburger," I was also teaching a select class, the Bill Plympton School of Animation, and I used the making of the film as an instructional tool. I had storyboarded the short, and I thought that the story was pretty strong, but when I put together the pencil test, the ending just sat there, like a wet noodle—the resolution was a failure.

And the class agreed that my ending totally sucked. I thought, let's go back to the beginning and see if we can bring something from the beginning full circle in the end. Someone in the class loved the idea of the mama cow coming back in the end. That totally resolved the ending—this young calf who loved his mother, rebelled, and got into big trouble was saved by his ever-loving mother. Ah, the power of a mother's love is the strongest force in the world! So there was the conflict not only with the butchers, but with his mother.

The mother coming back at the end also indicated that the story was over. The fable was complete, and the audience felt that every conflict in the film had come full circle and was resolved.

A great ending can save a bad film, but a boring ending can ruin a good film. I think that's because it's the last thing you remember about a film, so you walk out of the cinema thinking, "Wow, what a cool ending!" and not "What a mediocre film!"

"REJECTED" BY DON HERTZFELDT, 2000

Other Directors' Notes

I asked some of my great animator friends to list for me the most important elements for a successful film, and here's what they said.

Don Hertzfeldt ("Rejected", "Billy's Balloon")

"The film needs to be honest. Not just a project to get a three-picture deal from Hollywood. It should be from the heart."

Peter Lord (Aardman's *Chicken Run*):

"1. A well-developed bad character. 2. Surprising story points. 3. An ironic idea for a plot (example: a chicken breaking out of a POW camp). 4. A deeply-flawed hero."

Pat Smith ("Mask", "Delivery")

"Have a good ending. The best way to end a film is to simply give the main character what he or she wanted all along, but not in the way he/she could ever foresee. A solid ending will make your film very

"MASK" BY PAT SMITH, 2011

memorable, whereas a poor ending can ruin even the best imagery and story leading up to it.

Make all your ideas as simple as possible, and try to keep films short in length. Simplicity is king. All great things are simple. Expressing a simple idea/story will give you more time to concentrate on emotion, character, and technique. The story itself can hold you down if you allow it to boss you around.

Feel what you're animating. If you can *feel* it, you will be able to animate it well. Feel it stick, hit, slide, crack, stretch, etc. By feeling what you're animating,

you will be able to capture the emotion and timing … I'm talking about becoming the material you are creating. For example, right now, if I were to become a bomb, I would hunch down, put my hands in front of me like I'm mimicking a sphere … I would begin to shake as I feel the explosion coming. I would suck in slightly as to feel the anticipation, and BOOOOM! I would leap up as if all my guts were being sprayed across the walls!!! If you can do that, you will be a lot closer to capturing it when you animate it.

Concentrate on what comes before and after the action. The motion of a character before he or she performs the action is more important than the action itself. This is why the principle of anticipation is so vital to movement. Also, what happens directly after the action is also vital. Every action needs to be set up; the audience needs to be aware of the reason the character is taking the action, and they also need to know the thought process and emotions behind the reason. Put it this way: the way you throw a ball is not decided by the actual throw itself, but by the anticipation and setup of that throw.

Slow down and use subtle actions. Life is slower than you think, especially when it comes to acting. The audience needs time to see the character think. The most important actions aren't actions at all; they are thoughts. So slow down, use blinks, use small actions and motions that we do when we are in thought. Do we smack our lips before we drink? Do we let out a big sigh directly prior to making a decision? Be creative, act it out, take note of the smaller subtle actions you find yourself doing."

That's a very important question! There are a number of very obvious answers:

1. Myself

2. The distributors and acquisition people

3. The critics/judges

4. The festivals

5. My friends and family

6. Posterity

7. The audience

All of these answers are good ones, and to a certain extent, I make my films for all those on the list. But if you really want to know, the most important for me are #1 and #7.

Certainly, I need to sell my film—I need the money to keep making more films.

The critics are very important to the success of a film; a great review in *Variety* or the *New York Times* is extremely helpful for the success of a film. And the festivals are, for me, the first important stepping stone to getting the film out to the audiences. Of course, winning a major festival prize or getting an Oscar nomination is exceedingly important for a film's success, but that's not my ultimate goal.

I always love it when my friends and family like what I create. However, quite frankly, there are times when my family doesn't enjoy, appreciate, or understand my work.

I hope that my films have a long shelf life and that 100 years from now, people will still love and find humor in my work. But the two goals that dominate my need to make these films are to please myself and to please the audience.

Early in my animation career, I was obsessed with getting huge laughs and huge applause for my animated cartoons, so I would stick as many jokes as I possibly could into each film, theoretically to maximize the laughter quotient—the audience was god!

But as I matured, I found that when I put more of my own personality and emotion into a film, it becomes a more powerful film. So, to answer the original question, I'd say I make my film 50 percent for myself and 50 percent for the audience.

My friend, great Oregon poet Walt Curtis, once said to me, "Creating great work is what's important." I now think that's a very powerful statement. Don't worry about press, critics, film distributors, judges, agents, festivals, family, and friends. If you concentrate your energies on the work, people will discover it.

Comedy

If you've read my Dogma list, you know how humor is one of the key elements to my success.

"A day without laughter is a day wasted."

—CHARLIE CHAPLIN

Not only is laughter good for your soul and spirit; it's great for your body as well. Exercising the facial muscles that produce smiles keeps your face looking young. It's proven that laughter can cure cancer (check out Norman Cousin's 1979 book *Anatomy of an Illness*) and even help you live longer. In fact, morose people who don't watch cartoons tend to die at a very young age. Those are some of the reasons I like to write stories that result in a laughing audience. In fact, there's nothing cooler for me than sitting in the cinema when an audience breaks out in laughter from one of my films—I can witness everyone turning younger right before my eyes.

As I listen to people laugh, I feel a certain power over the audience—it's a god-like power that must be similar to what a great musician feels or an actor giving a great performance feels; they have the audience in their hands. But I feel like I'm making the world into children again. I'm the living embodiment of the Fountain of Youth.

So, how do you make people laugh?

They say that dying is easy, but making people laugh is hard. Therefore, I suffer fools … gladly. Really, I like to hear what fools say, because that may lead to a great bit of comedy.

In my humble opinion, it all comes down to sur-realism. People laugh when something happens that is a surprise, unexplained, or preposterous. But it has to be absurdly surreal.

I'll use my Guard Dog shorts as an example. The poor dog is always frustrated by his attempts to find a companion or master, and obviously he always fails. For the humor to work, he has to fail miserably and com-pletely. But it's the surprise and shock of how he fails, especially when it's so extreme and outrageous, that makes the films funny. The more absurd the contrast— the more shocking and unreal—the funnier it is. If it were an everyday kind of rejection, then it wouldn't be funny; it would become a sad drama, instead. But if it's totally crazy and bizarre, then we laugh.

Someone told me a story they'd heard about a Brazilian couple who came to New York to spend their honeymoon at the famous Plaza Hotel. They were so happy to be at the prestigious hotel that they began to bounce on the fancy bed like it was a trampoline. But they lost their balance and fell out of the penthouse window to their deaths below.

Now, that's a tragic story, but I couldn't help but laugh. Why was I laughing? It's a terrible tragedy, but the absurdity and surprise of the complete joy and happiness suddenly turning to fear and death is one of the hallmarks of great humor.

This phenomenon is true not just for cartoons, but also for writing. The only type of humor I can think of where surrealism doesn't come into play is puns, but I never thought that puns were all that funny anyway.

You'll notice that a lot of my jokes are set up using clichés. In most storytelling, clichés are evil, but in humor, they're golden. I learned this fact when I began my political strip, *Plympton*. The more common clichés were famous paintings, like Edward Munch's *The Scream*, which I used a lot because they were very eye-catching and already somewhat humorous.

So a great source of humor is found in clichés, but the really fresh humor is found in new clichés. I discovered that the concept of your life flashing before your eyes just before you die was an international cliché—I had thought it was just a weird concept shared by a large number of people.

Look, if we take the freeway, here, we can visit some nice trailer parks.

EXAMPLE OF A CARTOON USING THE CLICHÉ OF CYCLONES ALWAYS HITTING TRAILER PARKS

So I decided to make a gag cartoon out of that in a short film called "Sex and Violence," where a guy can't find his car keys. He looks everywhere and can't remember where he lost them. He decides that the only way to find them is to commit suicide, so his life will replay itself and he'll see where he last put his keys. Sure enough, the short gag was funny all over the world, as the cliché was universal. That's the kind of cliché that can lead to a great joke.

a fire hydrant, the hydrant pours water on the dog. You get the idea. There are hundreds of these ideas out there, waiting to be discovered, and the weirdest and most preposterous ideas will be the funniest.

I also like using clichés in my film titles. "The Cow Who Wanted to Be a Hamburger" plays on the cliché of all cows ending up at McDonald's.

"SEX AND VIOLENCE" SEGMENT, "THE LOST KEY", 1999

Another great source of humor is taking clichés and reversing them. For example, instead of a guy slipping on a banana peel, what about a banana slipping on a guy? Or, instead of a dog peeing on

VISUAL JUXTAPOSITION, UNPUBLISHED ILLUSTRATION, PEN AND INK, 1980

Another great category of humor is juxtaposition—in other words, slapping together two very contradictory elements. I'm sure you can think of dozens of clichéd or contradictory titles, such as "Why Hugh Hefner Can't Get Laid," "Auschwitz: The Happy Times," or even "Santa: The Fascist Years."

One great example of contradiction, of course, is Neil Simon's play *The Odd Couple*, which is about two men who have absolutely different lifestyles trying to live together. Or something like *The Beverly Hillbillies*, with country yokels living among very rich and cultured neighbors. Or, conversely, *Green Acres*, with rich snobs living on a farm.

I use this setup a lot; for example, in *Idiots and Angels*, an idiot guy *becomes* his opposite, an angel, so the conflict and contrast appears on the same guy, which opens up the story to lots of possibilities for humor.

Another rich vein of comedy is exaggeration: taking a gag and pushing it to the limits of believability. There's a lot more humor to something if you keep stretching it to these limits, which is what makes animation so great: the ability to really push for the edge. For example, in

"PUSH COMES TO SHOVE", 1991

my short film "Push Comes to Shove," two guys are having a fight and each is trying to harm the other. It was inspired by an old Laurel and Hardy routine, very deadpan, in which one of them would take an egg, lift the other one's hat, smash the egg on the top of his head, and replace the hat with nary a blink of the eye.

Well, I loved that routine, and I wondered what would happen if I took that concept and pushed it to the very extremes of personal pain and beyond. For example, one gag starts with one of the men stringing a rope through all of his opponent's facial orifices and then tying the rope to the bumper of an off-screen car. As the car takes off, we see that a large boulder was strapped to the rope off-screen, and the rock must now pass through every orifice in his head. Not a pleasant experience, but terrifically funny.

The capper to the funny bit is that the guy reacts with zero pain or emotion, making the gag doubly surreal and absurd. It's so exaggerated that it becomes impossible—but you just saw it—so you're forced into great amounts of laughter, I hope.

Character Development

A lot of writers claim that Disney invented character animation—in other words, cartoon characters that are full of dimension and personality. The so-called beginning point would be the seven dwarves in *Snow White*.

I disagree. I believe Winsor McCay's "Gertie the Dinosaur" was a fully developed, multidimensional character decades before Disney started infusing his characters with deeper personalities.

For many years, I was criticized for the lack of depth in my characters and for the perception that humor is more important to me than full personality development. Only over the last few years have I started to take more care to show multiple sides to the personages in my films. My first real experience in working on a film with more sensitivity and character development was when the great TV writer Dan O'Shannon (*Frasier, Modern Family*) asked me to direct a wonderful story he'd written called "The Fan and the Flower." He was extremely helpful

"THE FAN AND THE FLOWER", BILL PLYMPTON AND DAN O'SHANNON, 2005

by showing me how a good writer can get depths of emotion and sensitivity out of common household objects like a ceiling fan and a houseplant. The clincher was that after every screening, people would rush up to me crying, saying how this film moved them so deeply.

I wished I could thank them and tell them it was all my doing. But really, it was the genius of Dan O'Shannon that brought out all these emotions. So I said to myself, maybe I should try this scam—what a great and powerful way to make people love my films.

For example, the main character of *Idiots and Angels*, whom I call "Angel," is a lot more complicated than my usual animated stars. In fact, I sacrificed a lot of humor and violence to show the deeper sides of his personality.

I also believe that a lot of the success of my Guard Dog series comes from the dilemmas my dog always finds himself in, because people can identify with him. They say to themselves, "I'm similar to that dog, who's searching for love."

For those of you who haven't seen my Guard Dog series: it's predicated on the simple idea that everyone wants and needs love. This dog, who's basically an orphaned mutt, wants it so bad that he becomes much too eager to please—so much so that he ends up maiming or killing the object of his affection. In each short, he decides to give 100 percent of his love to someone, but by the end, he's completely heartbroken and depressed because he loved too much and drove away his lover. Yet he continues his search for a new companion.

It's great that people respond so well to the Guard Dog. He's become my Mickey Mouse, and even the simplest emotion or turn of his head evokes sympathy for this put-upon canine, which makes my job as a writer much easier when creating a film.

But just a little side note to my critics and fans: even though I seem to have matured and mellowed with *Idiots and Angels* and the Guard Dog series, I still hope to go back to my anarchic sex, violence, and gag-oriented films, because I love to make those, and I believe that audiences love to watch them.

Children versus Adults

Currently, all of the big money-making animated films are for kids. The big studios—Disney, DreamWorks, Pixar, Blue Sky, and Sony—all make "family" films, and they do a great job of it. So great, in fact, that they're able to top the box office reports every year.

Now, there's no way I can compete with those big guys. I don't have the money, the personnel, or the smarts. If I made a "family" film, I'd be squashed like a bug at the box office. And that's one of the reasons I decided to gear my films toward adult audiences. It's a niche that the great Ralph Bakshi pioneered for decades, but now that he's retired, I hope to take up his place as the premier creator of animation for adults.

Another reason I've decided to avoid children's cartoons is because of my background. Ever since my college days, when I made cartoons for the university's paper, I've wanted to reflect my own thoughts and feelings through my humor.

NOTICE THE SIMILARITIES OF ALL OF THE ADULT DESIGNS VERSUS THE CHILD DESIGNS.

When I moved to New York, most of my survival was dependent on cartoons that I did for all of the adult magazines like *Screw*, *Hustler*, *Adelina*, *Penthouse*, *Cheri*, *Playboy*, and *National Lampoon*. And I thrived on it, because these were based on my everyday thoughts, not toys, kids playing games, and singing animals. No, I was thinking about love, jealousy, cheating, death, revenge, sex, hatred, and all of the seven deadly sins.

Besides, these topics were much more interesting to me.

I believe that the old refrain "Write what you know" is very true. Well, I'm not a kid, and I don't have any kids, so why should I make films for kids? I want to make films in which I bring up serious topics in a humorous or wacky way. And I believe that animation is the perfect art form to recreate these darker, deeper stories, because there are no limits in animation. No actors complaining when their heads are cut off or when they have to do impossible action sequences—I like that.

Just so you know, I actually have made films that are appropriate for kids—*The Tune*, "Gary Guitar," "12 Tiny Christmas Tales," "The Fan and the Flower," and "The Cow Who Wanted to Be a Hamburger"—and all of these films were very successful, but still I felt like I had to restrain myself. I had to control my free-spirited ways, and be sure not to offend anyone – which brings me to the next topic.

People often ask me why my films are so full of gratuitous sex and violence. Do you know what the root word for "gratuitous" is? It's "gratify." I want to gratify the audience, and I believe that's what my films supply—gratification.

So I'm proud to have sex and violence in my films. Is it offensive that animation, long the medium of Disney, should also show the naked human body or sensuality? It seems only natural: from Mae West and Betty Boop to Marilyn Monroe and Jessica Rabbit, Americans have always loved sex in their films.

As for violence, let me tell you a little story. One day, I was running to catch a NYC subway train, and I turned my head to check out a movie poster and smacked right into a big steel pillar. The typical New

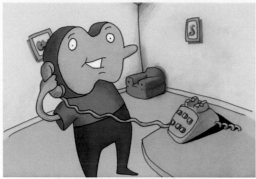

"GARY GUITAR", PAINTED CEL, 2006

Yorkers standing by saw this and broke into loud laughter. As my face turned red from the impact, I thought, "How could these people be so cold-hearted and find amusement in my pain and misfortune? How rude!"

But then I replayed my accident in my brain, and I thought, "Wow, that was a pretty stupid move on my part. What a dummy I am!" and I started laughing, and the pain in my throbbing head wenta

And that's what I think happens when people watch my films—the comic violence is so exaggerated and absurd that people laugh at it, and that laughter is a tonic for whatever is bothering you.

Live Action versus Animation

Why is it that animation is so popular, yet seems to get no respect from Hollywood? Why is it that everyone knows who the big live-action directors are, but no one can identify the directors of animated films? Yet these films make billions of dollars.

Other than Walt Disney, John Lasseter, and Tim Burton, most animation directors seem to be obscure artists working behind the scenes and making brilliant masterpieces. But that's okay; eventually, people will realize the true greats of animation.

During the 1990s, I took a little detour to the town of live action and created three features: *J. Lyle* (1994), *Guns on the Clackamas* (1995), and *Walt Curtis: The Peckerneck Poet* (1997). All three were complete disasters.

I think the reason I belly-flopped in live action was that there were certain limitations with live actors that I never had to confront with animation—things like twisting an actor's head around 360 degrees … SAG has rules about that.

Also, I think my audience preferred for me to stay with animation; they couldn't accept Bill Plympton as a live-action director. By the way, these films are available on DVD if you want to see them.

The great thing about animation for me is that it fully recreates the bizarre images in my head. Live action can never do that. And I think that people want to see something fresh, something they've never seen before. They're like kids; they like the sense of wonder and unpredictability that can be found only in animation.

Animation is the greatest art form in the world! It rocks!

Censorship versus Self-Censorship

Fortunately, these days censorship is not as big an issue as it was in the past. Thanks to cable and the Internet, there are many more avenues of distribution for work that might offend certain people.

Having said that, I have had a few of my films censored.

When my film *The Tune* was released by October Films in 1992, I wanted to use a promotional quote from my great friend, *The Simpsons* creator Matt Groening: " 'The Tune' would make Bart Simpson laugh his ass off!" Sure enough, the *New York Times* refused to run the ad in their paper unless we removed the word "ass."

CENSORED SHOT FROM *I MARRIED A STRANGE PERSON*, 1997

Another time was when my animated feature *I Married a Strange Person* was released by Lionsgate Films. This film was probably the most transgressively wacky film I've ever made. Blockbuster Video said they wouldn't sell the film unless I removed four shots from the sex scenes—and even today, when you buy the film on DVD, it's still the censored version. I do plan to release a Director's Cut at some point and return the film to its original sleazy form.

But what is really important is self-censorship. I don't believe it to be a particularly bad thing—in fact, self-censorship is very important for the success of a film.

I did a commercial once for the Oregon Lottery, for a game called BlackJack, in which a man stuck his hand under a lawn mower to retrieve a winning scratch-off ticket that had blown away, and they were afraid that kids all over Oregon would start sticking their hands under mowers, looking for winning lottery tickets. They yanked the spot off the air after just three days.

When I'm looking to distribute my films, I need to identify my audience. So when I write the story or make the storyboards, I keep thinking in the back of my mind about the film's audience and how they'll react to things.

And it's not necessarily the sex or the violence; it can also be about the characters, such as how they react or what they say. I'm always looking to be provocative with my stories, but if they turn people off, then they're not going to be successful. So it's a form of self-censorship.

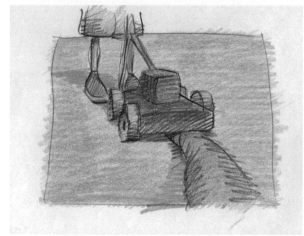

YANKED OREGON LOTTERY BLACKJACK AD, 1992

Chapter 6

CHARACTER DESIGN

ANDY WACHOWSKI, ME, AND GEOFFREY DARROW AT COMIC-CON 2004

The great graphic novel artist Geoffrey Darrow (the visual creative force behind the Matrix trilogy) once told me that when he was in Australia working on one of the Matrix films, one of his designers was asked to create some new storyboards for an added scene. The designer in question was a very highly paid production designer on the film, but he begged out of doing the storyboards by saying he couldn't draw. He couldn't draw? How the hell did he get that job? He said he was great at computer animation, knew all the programs, was a whiz at programming, but knew zilch about drawing the human body.

What the hell's going on? I've heard that a lot of art schools are dropping life-drawing classes to make way for more computer classes. What? Life-drawing is the basis of all art, and now they're graduating students that can't draw?!

Even at my age, I still attend life-drawing classes, and I sketch at home from images on TV or on the subway to keep my skills sharp. Please, dear readers, never stop drawing. If I were the Wachowski brothers, I would have fired that dumb production designer's ass.

This chapter is my introduction to character design, the job of the best artists in the world. Here are the elements that I feel are the most important for great visual characters.

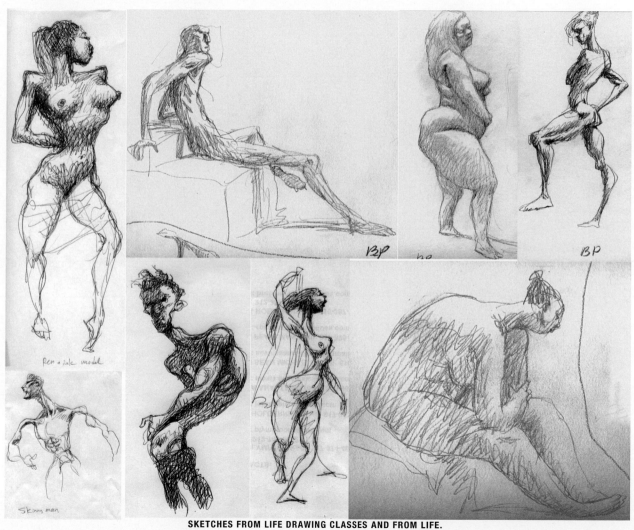

Pen + ink model

Skinny man

SKETCHES FROM LIFE DRAWING CLASSES AND FROM LIFE.

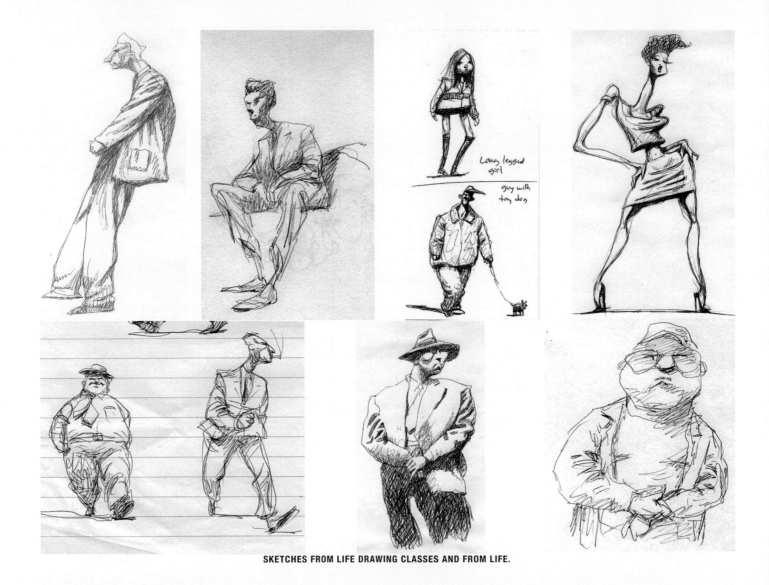

Long legged
girl

guy with
tiny dog

SKETCHES FROM LIFE DRAWING CLASSES AND FROM LIFE.

Strong Personality

The great thing about being involved in animation is that you get to play God. What the audience sees on the screen is a manifestation of what is inside your imagination.

Unlike a live-action director, you are not forced to work with only the actors who are available—you get to create new characters that are yours alone. They are unique, different; maybe there have never been characters like them before—what a thrill!

But there are certain rules to follow with your characters. They should reflect the personality of the creation in the story, and they must visually embody the elements of their souls, so there is no confusion in the viewer's eye about what each character represents. Also, as you leave the cinema, that personality should be alive in your brain like it was someone in your real life, such as a neighbor or a relative.

In fact, when I create a design for a character, I often look to real life for reference. I watch people for their movements, body positions, their manners, and their subtleties—how they look with different emotions.

All of these elements build strong personalities.

Dynamic Shapes

For me, dynamic shapes are the most important part of character design. The shape or silhouette of a character truly defines his or her effectiveness.

I see a lot of student films in which the characters are basically rectangular stubs, and I feel no empathy or emotion towards them. It's the shape of the character that brings out the emotion.

But what is a good shape?

In college, I had a design teacher named Arvid Orbeck, a wonderfully tall Norwegian who had fought Hitler's Nazis as part of the WWII underground resistance. He suggested that we always be aware of shapes and design in everyday life.

For example, during lunch, when you're sitting at your table, and in front of you is your fork, napkin, salt shaker, a sugar packet, whatever—take these objects, move them around on the table, and see how many interesting designs and shapes you can make. These shapes don't have to mean or symbolize anything; they just have to be pleasing to the eye in some way. This is an excellent way to hone your composition skills. It's quick, easy, and cheap.

You'd be surprised, though, how moving shapes around on a table can lead to making characters that have personalities and drama and can even tell a story (if you want to add a voice-over).

Another "secret" technique I like to employ is to keep the shapes triangular. I don't know why, but I find characters made out of squares (or rectangles) and circles very boring compared to triangles. Maybe it's just me, but triangles just seem to be more dynamic— they subconsciously put motion into the design. Look at the human face and how much cooler it is when it follows a triangular format; the square or circle looks so bland and emotionless.

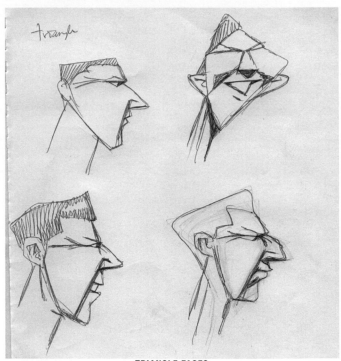

TRIANGLE FACES

Another great idea is to keep the body, object, or figure off balance. Balance denotes rest, stability, and boredom; something out of balance suggests conflict, movement, and unpredictability and is thus more fascinating.

A good character design should work in a close-up shot as well as on a distant horizon. That shape should be so distinctive that the audience will be able to identify it from 100 yards away—now that's a great character design!

NOTICE THE CHARACTER PROFILE READ WHETHER THEY ARE LARGE OR TINY: ROD FROM *HAIR HIGH* (2004)

Simplicity

Another important ingredient in character design is simplicity—it follows naturally that if your character reads well in silhouette, why bother putting a lot of distracting detail on the character? I see a lot of cartoon characters with tons of detail—intricate hair designs, clothes with excessive patterns, lots of jewelry, too much facial hair, and every feature of the face done in extravagant detail. And often these features either contradict each other or battle each other for attention. I know I've said that conflict is the basis for great story, but please don't have the conflict take place on a character's design.

For my needs, I like to keep the identifying features down to about two or three distinctive elements—perhaps a particular hair design, one strong facial element, or a unique body shape. That's all you really need for a great character design.

Line of Action

Look through the terrific book titled *Animation* by the brilliant Preston Blair. He talks a lot about "line of action" in a character. This term means that one should be able to draw a simple line through the character, and it should be a smooth, simple line that defines the position and shape of the character with no superfluous angles or wasted tangents. This guideline is important to give the audience a mental picture and clean memory of the characters.

Once you get to the animation of your characters, continue to use the line of action. It works in all parts of the film—romance, action, humor, violence, and tragedy. It makes it easier for the eye to follow the story and appreciate the characters.

LINE OF ACTION

EVOLUTION OF CHARACTER DESIGN OF ELLA FROM *CHEATIN'*

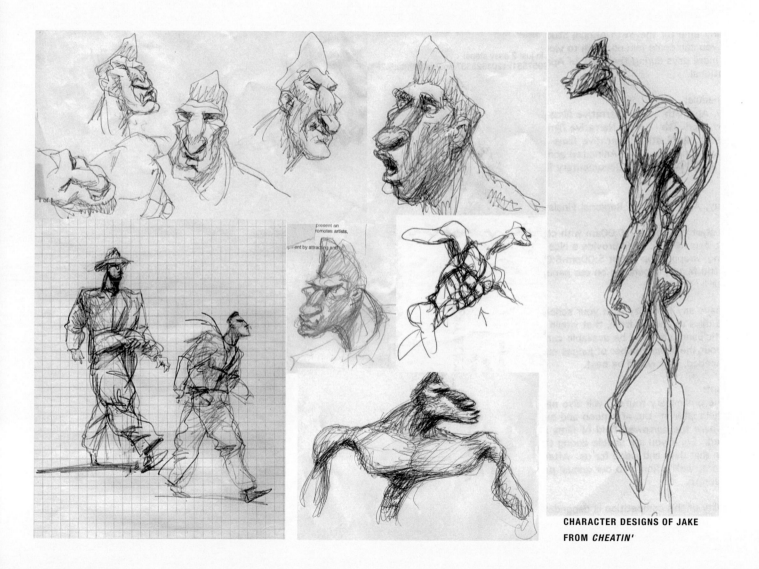

**CHARACTER DESIGNS OF JAKE
FROM *CHEATIN'***

**EVOLUTION OF CHARACTER
DESIGN OF EL MERTO
FROM *CHEATIN'***

MISCELLANEOUS DESIGNS FROM *CHEATIN'*

VARIOUS CHARACTER DESIGNS OF HITMAN FROM *CHEATIN'*

ARCHITECTURAL DESIGNS FROM *CHEATIN'*

CAR DESIGNS FROM *CHEATIN'*

40's car grill

Pushing the Eye Around

PUSHING THE EYE AROUND

You're going to hear a lot in this book about my theory of "pushing the eye around." It's nothing new, really—a lot of artists have talked about it before.

A while back, I was at a Q&A after a certain film screening, and the director was talking about how he wanted the film to manipulate the audience. A young female student felt offended that the director would dictate how the audience should feel. I guess she felt controlled—she wanted to be able to interpret the film in her own way. She must have preferred vague, abstract storytelling. Ambiguity and mystery are great for storytelling, but confusion is not—confusion is my nemesis!

It's my belief that the audience goes into a cinema wanting to be manipulated and controlled. In fact, one of the greatest manipulative films is *Jaws*—boy, do we get manhandled in that one.

There are many ways to push and control the viewers' eyes. Just like a magician uses distraction to make sure you don't see his sleight of hand, the animator wants to control the eye to help tell the story that's there in the storyboard or script. So the character design should reflect this control of the audience's vision.

If the character is a strong guy, do you want to concentrate on his abs, or his hair? If the woman has a strong personality, do you want to emphasize her shoulders or her feet? If a child is a bit manic, make sure people see his eyes; this might seem elementary, but the magic trick is to deemphasize the other parts of the body. Again, as I said, just concentrate on two or three factors of the character, letting the others be much more subdued and in the background. You can do this with color, outlines, lighting, texture, detailed shading, or just plain arrangement.

It's great playing God and controlling people's vision.

Be sure that all of the characters have a consistent look. No matter what technique you use—computer, pencil, Sharpie, Flash, stop-motion, and so on—all characters should look like they're from the same film. You should keep the style consistent: nothing's worse than characters that look like they're from a different movie. Well, actually there are things worse than that, like having an air conditioner fall on your head, but that shouldn't affect your film.

However, I believe that once you've established the character and you have your two or three strong identifiers, you'll be able to distort the drawings for emotional effect, and the audience will still know it's them. You can change a character's size, his body proportions, even his colors, and it's my bet that the audience will still accept them—try it!

Over the last five years, from "Guard Dog" to "Horn Dog", the look of my dog character has changed, yet people still love the dog and accept him as the consistently lovable loser he always is.

What Not To Do

TOP: WHAT NOT TO DO—A CHARACTER WITH TOO MANY EXTREME FACIAL CHARACTERISTICS AND LOUD CLOTHING. BOTTOM: CHARACTERS WITH ACCEPTABLE EXTREME FACIAL CHARACTERISTICS

I get a lot of students coming by my studio, and I look at their work, and see so many drawings that just *drive me crazy*! Here are my top no-nos in character design:

1. Please don't draw big hands. I drew big hands once for a week and then I realized how stupid it was. Back in the 1930s, when Mickey Mouse was popular, it was okay to draw big, gloved hands, but it's now almost a century later—so enough with the big hands. It looks like the artist is either extremely immature or stuck in the 1930s.

2. Big, booted feet. See #1. Grown-ups all wear well-designed shoes, and small feet look so much cooler on a character than clod-hoppers do. Big feet draw attention to themselves, and I'm sure the basics of the story are not dependent on a man's giant shoes.

3. Big noses. Some people believe that if a character has a big nose, then he's automatically funny. I tend to think he's got a humongous cold in his nose, and this is again a mark of an amateur. Way back in the early days of cartooning, a big nose was a way to make people laugh. But just like people tripping on a banana peel, the joke's been worn out. That funny ship has sailed; we must find more original ways to make people laugh, hopefully with something connected to the story.

4. Please stop showing me animé and manga! I gave up teaching because everyone was copying Japanese artwork. If I see another Japanese character from young students, I'll strangle that person.

5. Loud clothing. Please do not put wild, vivid, colorful patterns in your character's clothing, even if he is a clown. My eye gets totally confused when the clothing dominates the screen. No plaid, please.

I look to some character designers for inspiration. These guys, in every film, create vivid, original, amazing designs that just blow me away. Check out Peter DeSeve, Carter Goodrich, Carlos Nine, Peter Chung, Heinz Edelmann, Will Eisner, and Winsor McCay.

The character above has all of the traits of a bad drawing, but characters with just one unusual trait are okay.

Chapter 7

STORYBOARDING

It's my strong opinion that if you've got a great storyboard, you're going to have a great film. There are many important decisions that are resolved in the storyboard process:

1. Story: All story issues are resolved in the storyboard.

2. Editing: All the cuts and sequences should be decided at the storyboard stage.

3. Pacing: Can be decided at this stage.

4. Composition and design of the frame

5. Action: The movement and flow of action sequences

6. Backgrounds: Rough versions of the backgrounds

7. Layouts: For me, the storyboards are as good as layouts.

8. Character design: Character and prop visuals can be resolved here.

9. Camera angles

10. Camera lens: Wide shots, deep focus, zooms, etc.

11. Fashion: Clothing, costumes, accessories, hair

12. Special effects: Explosions, cross-dissolves, camera tricks, etc.

13. Color design

14. Sound cues

15. Music suggestions

16. Dialogue

17. Shadows

And on top of all that, I use the storyboards to make an animatic (like a storyboard on DVD with music and voices) to help get a good feel for how the film will look when it's finished. The animatic can also be used for promotion and demonstration purposes and shown to potential buyers, investors, or distributors.

I know some people think that storyboards are a waste of time, but to me, they are indispensable. In fact, when I'm drawing the animation, I like to put the storyboard on top of my desk and, starting on page one, work my way through the whole story using my sketches as the layouts and inspiration. That way, the film is made in sequence.

I usually create an extremely rough storyboard first by drawing thumbnail sketches that are very loose. I then review, edit, and redraw the thumbnails into much larger storyboards, six to an 8½" by 11" page. And I try to put as much information into the drawings as possible. Because I go from the sketches to

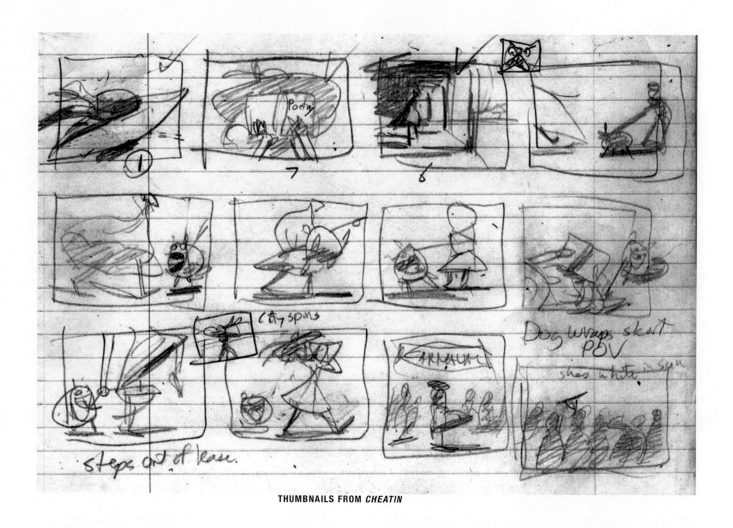

THUMBNAILS FROM *CHEATIN*

the animation, it really helps to have as much detail as possible worked out before I animate. I like to include clothing, details, shadows, effects, background characters, backgrounds—anything that helps tell the story. Like I said earlier, the storyboards become my layouts.

Often I'll include a number of storyboard drawings in one shot, especially if there's an important development or transformation. Or, a chase or fight sequence may involve a number of different bits of action. So, occasionally one or two pages will encompass one whole film shot. But usually one page (six drawings) covers approximately 15 to 20 seconds of action. That means that each shot of my film usually lasts about 2 to 3 seconds.

It bugs the hell out of me when film executives refuse to look at storyboards and review only scripts. But there are a number of executives who do understand and love storyboards. So often, I'll use the storyboards—or, better still, the animatic—to sell the film project.

I love animatics! Sometimes called "story reels" or "Leica reels," they're basically comic books with sound, and because I've done a number of graphic novels, animatics are kind of like the next step. I usually hire a sound person to slot in the dialogue and music, and voilà—the film is there! The film executives can thus get a better idea of what the film will look, sound, and feel like. It's a much more complete version of the potential finished picture.

Also, if I'm shipping out a number of shots to other animators (which I rarely do) or I want to show the film to voice artists, sound designers, musicians, or any other postproduction people, the animatic is essential.

What do you put in a storyboard?

There are two questions I ask when making the individual shots:

1. Does this shot advance the story?

2. Is this shot entertaining?

In a perfect world, it would be great to have the same shot both advance the story *and* be entertaining. In other words, while someone is talking, I try to give him some business to occupy his hands or body. That helps define his character or bring some humor to the story.

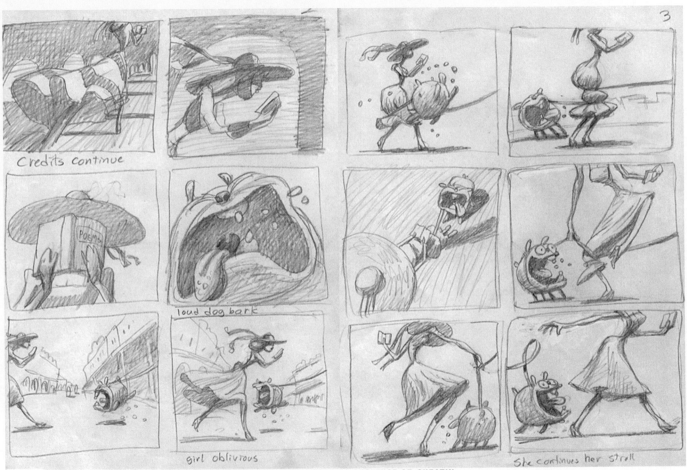

FINISHED STORYBOARDS FROM OPENING SEQUENCE OF *CHEATIN*

Chapter 8

VOICES

As most of you know, many of my films have no voices. For me, the storytelling is in the visuals—my films "25 Ways to Quit Smoking," "Push Comes to Shove," "One of Those Days," all my "Dog" films, "The Cow Who Wanted to Be a Hamburger," and *Idiots and Angels* were all voiceless.

There are a number of reasons I don't use dialogue in some of my films:

Reason 1: Films with dialogue are a lot harder to sell in the foreign territories. The cost of subtitling or dubbing is quite expensive, and often that expense will determine whether the film is bought in that territory.

Reason 2: Animating to lip-sync is very slow, difficult, and tedious. It sucks up a lot of energy and time, and it's not a discipline I enjoy doing.

Reason 3: I'm not a very good dialogue writer. I wish I were, and I hope to get better at it, but I almost flunked English Composition in college.

To me, the image is God. I respond to the visuals, whether it's a painting or photography or a film. That's what gets me excited! Visuals are more poetic and speak to the soul. By comparison, words seem to always be explaining things, not carrying the heart of the story. I want to tell a story visually, not verbally.

However, a majority of my films have included dialogue, and I love good dialogue. If an animated film is properly cast and voiced, it's a joy to hear.

How do you decide which films have dialogue and which don't?

Boy, that's a tough question. I never really thought of that before.

I guess I would answer it by saying that my preference is to not use dialogue, but if the characters seem to be telling me that they want to talk, then I've got to listen to them. I suppose it's usually the complexity of the story that determines whether I use dialogue. Also, I've found that television pretty much demands dialogue; I've never seen a TV show that didn't have words. But maybe I'll make the first one—who knows?

Also, you may ask why the voices come before the animation. Ever since films have included sound, the voices in animated films have dictated how the characters move and talk. It's a hell of a lot easier to match the drawings to a voice than to record a voice to match up with a moving mouth. Although the Italians have been very successful in matching dialogue to action, in most Hollywood animated films it's much easier to have all of the voices recorded before going into animation.

Casting

I find my voice actors in many different ways—when I go to the movies, the theater, or comedy clubs, I always make notes of the great voice talent. Also, I use my sound designer as a great resource for good voices. He'll look at my animatic to find voices that he considers appropriate.

My sound engineer and sound designer work with dozens of voice actors every day, and they have certain favorites that are very talented, professional, and easy to work with. That last one, "easy to work with," is very important.

I used to use my friends for voices, and although they could do great voices at a party with a few drinks in them, when they got in front of a microphone, they would often freeze up. So it is important to get experienced actors or professionals.

And that brings up the next decision: SAG (Screen Actors Guild) or non-SAG? If you're working on a big production, with loads of money, then it's definitely important to work with union actors. They are (usually) famous and will help attract the audience into the theaters.

I did that with my animated feature *Hair High,* and here is the story behind that film. I was in a bar with my cousin, the great actress Martha Plimpton, commiserating about the lack of success I had with the release of *Mutant Aliens.* She said that maybe she could make a few calls to her friends and get some big names to do voices in my next feature, *Hair High*. I said, "Great!" but I wasn't expecting much.

However, she called me the next week and read off the list of actors she had been able to contact for me: Sarah Silverman, Keith and David Carradine (her father and uncle, respectively), Beverly D'Angelo, Eric Gilliland, Ed Begley, Jr., Peter Jason, and Matthew Perry—wow! I couldn't believe my luck. I thought *Hair High* would definitely sell big-time.

At the same time, my office manager, John Holderried, made some phone calls and was able to get in touch with Justin Long and Michael Showalter, who were both eager to get involved too. I booked a sound studio in Los Angeles and another one in New York, and then we started to arrange the paperwork.

Working with SAG was something of a nightmare; a big Hollywood production has lawyers to deal with all the paperwork, but as my studio had only four employees, poor John Holderried had to deal with all of the SAG red tape.

MARTHA PLIMPTON AS MISS CRUMBLES (*HAIR HIGH*)

The first problem was the SAG rates were too high—they would have broken my budget. SAG has a low-budget agreement for independent films, but it didn't apply to animation. At first they didn't believe that anyone could make an animated feature for under $500,000—I guess no one had ever done it before—not using big Hollywood talent, anyway. John had to argue with the formidable bureaucracy at SAG for months to convince them that I could make an animated feature for $200,000 so that we could finally get an indie pay scale.

KEITH CARRADINE AS JOJO (*HAIR HIGH*)

The actors were all willing to take a pay cut because they knew it was a very low-budget film and that I was paying for it out of my own pocket. Fortunately, they all thought it would be fun to do; most of them had never worked in animation before. But SAG almost didn't sign off on the operation. In the end, they gave us a waiver for each cast member to sign, and *Hair High* became the first animated feature made under SAG's low-budget agreement.

The second problem was the mountain of paperwork: the contracts that needed to be filled out. Forms that asked things like, "Did you search for female Native American voice artists in the casting process?" No, I didn't have the budget to scour tribal reservations looking for voice talent. Plus, I already knew who I wanted to cast, thanks to Martha.

Third, the day before our final voice-over session in Los Angeles, I got a call from Matthew Perry's agent, saying that even though Matthew was gung-ho for the project, the agent was afraid that we'd use Matthew's big name unfairly to promote the film. Uh-oh! I freaked out and called Martha with the bad news, and Martha—brilliant trouper that she is—called her buddy, Dermot Mulroney, who stepped in on one day's notice.

The great news was that it was a total delight to work with such professionals. I paid them below scale, but they were so committed and dedicated to the job that it was one of the most enjoyable projects I'd ever done. And a lot of that is because of my great friend, Martha Plimpton.

Unfortunately, the fantastic voices never really helped me sell the film. It never got picked up by a distribution company, so in the end I wasn't really convinced that hiring top-notch voice talent makes a film much more sellable.

After that letdown, I decided to not use voices in my next feature, *Idiots and Angels*; to my surprise, that film got a much better response than *Hair High* and did a whole lot better in terms of distribution and sales. Also, the budget was half as large.

Unless I get a big Hollywood contract that allows me to hire big-name stars, I believe I'll stick with nonunion voice actors when casting my features. It's just a lot less hassle that way. And when you're making a film with a small staff, the simpler, the better.

I'll now describe my procedure for creating voices for one of my films. I'm now casting voices for a new film called "Tiffany," and there are about 15 speaking roles in the film. (This "Tiffany" project is a very long, serialized feature that's way beyond my current financial resources. However, if I'm not able to make a sale, I suppose I'll have to resort to self-financing it over time.)

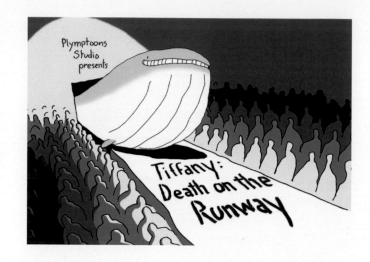

First, I make a list of the characters with notes about what voice qualities I'm looking for, along with a drawing of each character. Obviously, only a few of the characters are lead roles, and those are the ones that have to be perfectly cast.

In this case, I want to make a short version of the feature film first, as sort of a trailer to help get financing for the feature film. So I choose a small excerpt of the story that would work as a short film that I could enter in film festivals. Ideally, this would get the project some publicity, and I could also use it as an example to show people what the finished feature will look like.

I begin to call some of my usual voice actors—people I've worked with and had good experiences with and people who I think are appropriate for the job. I also call my sound designers for recommendations. I bring some of them into my studio for auditions to see how they might fit with my idea for the character.

I give them a page from the script and a drawing of their character, and then I sit with each actor and discuss the personality of the character and the feeling I want. I'll maybe even try to mimic the voice myself—although I'm terrible at doing voices—or I'll think of a famous actor's voice that they can use as a model.

It's really important for me to close my eyes and imagine my animated character with each actor's voice as they are reading their lines. Often, watching the actor read is very distracting, and the actor's appearance has absolutely nothing to do with the quality of their voice.

When I find an actor I like, I ask the actor if he or she would like to do a scratch (rough) reading of all of the character's lines for my pilot short. This way, I can see how the actor's voice will work with the animated character, and I can edit this pilot together to try and raise funds for the film.

SARAH SILVERMAN AS CHERI (*HAIR HIGH*)

I usually offer the (non-SAG) voice actors around $100 for an hour's recording, and they usually accept, for a number of reasons:

1. It's great experience.

2. They can put on their resume that they worked with Bill Plympton (I know that sounds like I'm bragging, but the actors usually tell me that this helps them).

3. Who knows: this project could turn into the next *Simpsons*, and they could be walking on Easy Street for the rest of their life.

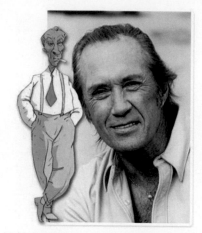

DAVID CARRADINE AS MR. SNERZ (*HAIR HIGH*)

For the pilot film, I usually record in my studio, and we use the microphone I have there. It's a lot easier (and cheaper) than going to a studio, and it sounds quite good. If the pilot is a hit, which I hope it is, I'll call my sound designer and ask him to set up a voice-record session, booking a studio for two or three days so that we have enough time to record all of the actors.

There are a number of things I look for in a sound engineer. Obviously, the sound engineer must have a good ear. He or she must be inventive: sometimes, the craziest sound works the best. Sound engineers should

have a sense of humor, not only because of my work, but because often when there is a problem, tensions can rise and tempers can flare; in these situations, you need someone cool and professional.

Sound engineers should be technically proficient with all of the digital programs and technology involved in recording. Finally, they should know my work and understand what I'm trying to do, and they should also be easy to work with.

As for the sound studio, I don't want a big expensive studio with a bunch of pinball machines, a game room, and a full buffet for the actors. These studios are for advertising agency clients and big Hollywood films. I'm drawn to the simple padded sound rooms with two or three microphones, script stands, and a video screen so that the actors can see the animatic or pencil test as they read their lines.

After we do a few simple rehearsals, then we usually move into the recording booth and record about four or five takes of each line. Usually the last one is the keeper. I mark that one as my "select," and we move on. I've found that if you do more than ten takes of a line, the entire meaning of the words can get lost, everyone gets frustrated and tired, and it becomes an exercise in futility.

I usually record the actors separately; I rarely do recordings in tandem, because often there is bleed-over. In other words, one microphone can pick up the other actor's voice, and then it's not a clean reading. However, if I'm recording a crowd or a group conversation, or if I'm recording a song, then it's good to have more than one microphone.

One last bit of advice: record the actors on video while they're reading their lines, for a few good reasons. For one thing, I use this as reference footage; it helps when I'm animating to be able to see how the actors moved and gestured when acting out the dialogue. Also, when putting the DVD together, it's very interesting to include footage from the voice-over sessions as an extra feature.

For the DVD release of *Hair High,* we included footage from Ed Begley, Jr. (hilarious), and Sarah Silverman (wonderful) and they really helped to make the DVD a collector's item.

DERMOT MULRONEY AS ROD (*HAIR HIGH*)

ED BEGLEY, JR., AS REVEREND SIDNEY CHEDDAR (*HAIR HIGH*)

SARAH SILVERMAN AND ME AT A SOUND SESSION

Chapter 9

ANIMATION

Now for the most fun chapter—and this is the part I was born for: *animation*! You'll be seeing a lot of sketches and examples in this chapter, because I'm so much more comfortable showing what I mean rather than talking about it. So fasten your seat belts: it's going to be an exciting ride.

Influences

There are many great animators; in this chapter, I will give you a list of my favorites. I think it's important to study the best; even now, I try to learn from the greats of the past and those working today. I want to continue to learn and grow, and one of the best ways is to study from the masters and to discover why animation is such a powerful art form. (Remember, there are a lot of fabulous animators that I'm leaving off this list, but listed here are the ones I look at the most.)

- First (and maybe the greatest) is Winsor McCay, animator of "Gertie the Dinosaur," "Little Nemo," and "The Sinking of the Lusitania"

(brilliant!). This is the guy who really influenced Walt Disney to become an animator.

In fact, as I write this, I'm trying to contemporize one of McCay's forgotten classics, "The Flying House." I discovered this film when I got a collection of his works, and I wondered why I'd never seen this amazing film before. Well, probably because it's hard to watch—it was produced in 1921 and runs about 13 minutes; what makes

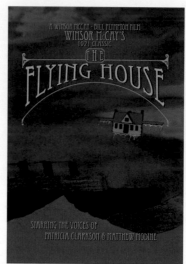

POSTER FOR "THE FLYING HOUSE" PROJECT

it hard to watch is the presence of loads of word balloons and intertitles. Plus, it's black and white, silent, and there are lots of imperfections in the print (scratches, dust, reflections).

So I took it upon myself to fix all of these problems. I've cleaned up the surface so that it's not all dirty and scratched. I've added color, gotten rid of all the captions, and hired Matthew Modine and Patricia Clarkson to voice the dialogue. Plus, I hired musicians and sound designers to create a soundtrack.

Without all of the written copy, the film is now down to a clean, speedy seven minutes, and it's a joy to watch. I know purists will criticize me for tampering with a masterpiece—well, that masterpiece had been sadly, but understandably, ignored and it's my goal to show young animators and the general public how great and brilliant Winsor McCay's films are.

(Sorry for that diversion—I'll continue now with my pantheon of great animators.)

- Milt Kahl: One of Disney's "Nine Old Men," and to me, one of the great draftsmen of all time.
- Preston Blair: I've talked about him before, but just check out his wonderful "Red Hot Riding Hood" animation, directed by the great Tex Avery. To me, dancing women are the hardest sequences to draw—I find them almost impossible without a model—and he did it out of his head! Wow!
- Rod Scribner, whose famous "Coal Black and de Sebben Dwarfs" (directed by Bob Clampett) is a masterpiece of animation and distortion.
- Hayao Miyazaki: Created some of the most beautiful animation ever. My favorites are *Porco Rosso* and *Princess Mononoke*.
- Joanna Quinn: One of the purest draftswomen alive today—her artwork is phenomenal.
- Michael Dudok de Wit: Animator of "Father and Daughter."
- Frédéric Back: Animator of "The Man Who Planted Trees."
- Glen Keane: The great Disney animator.

The great animators, in my opinion, are the artists who can magically fill their characters with a rich, believable soul and make them forever compelling. It's much more than great draftsmanship, although that helps—it's the power to tell a great story with rich, fascinating characters and to tell it in a new and unique way.

That's what I'm attempting to do with each film, and perhaps when I'm 90, I will have succeeded . . . I hope!

Techniques

The good news is that there are a multitude of style options available for young animators today—and there seem to be more developing every year. The only limits to the techniques are the artists' imaginations. Of course, the computer has aided greatly to the wide variety of styles in animation. Here are some of my favorites:

- CG (computer graphics animation): This includes Maya, used in the great Pixar and Blue Sky Films
- Flash: As seen on *Adult Swim*
- Cel animation: Used by most of the Japanese animators, including Miyazaki
- Stop-motion puppets: Tim Burton, Henry Selick, Laika Studios
- Claymation: Nick Park of the *Wallace & Gromit* series
- Stop-motion: Jan Svankmajer
- Oil on glass: The great Alexander Petrov
- Paper/cut-out: Michael Ocelot, Lotte Reiniger
- Drawn animation: This obviously is my favorite, as I grew up drawing and spent 20 years as an illustrator; I love the look, and I'll probably stick with this style of 2D art
- Pixillation: Norman McLaren, Juan Pablo Zaramello

ART STYLES ARE FUN TO PLAY WITH; SEE HOW MANY DIFFERENT ONES YOU CAN COME UP WITH.

There are, of course, a myriad of other styles—like sand painting, pin screen, collage, and mixed media. But for this book, as it's about animating like Bill Plympton, I'm going to concentrate on my 2D drawing style, which includes various art utensils like colored pencils, graphite pencils, and Sharpies.

Animation Secrets

If you were to visit my studio in New York City, you'd see a large traditional animation board with the clear plastic animation disk in the middle, shelves for the stacks of drawings, my trusty mirror by my side, and electronic pencil sharpener, and of course my ubiquitous iPod for music (more about that later). It's definitely old school, and it looks like it might be straight out of the Fleischer days, except for the iPod.

I have a box of Ticonderoga #2s and a couple of old coffee cans filled with Prismacolor pencils—nothing radical or cutting edge about that. What's really important is the 40 years of constant practice in drawing. That makes the difference.

I'm going to go on a small rant now, so get ready . . .

I believe that one of the most important keys to my success, such as it is, is the visual storytelling—and how did I get to be such a great visual storyteller? By studying drawing. I still take life-drawing classes, and as I draw the model, I try to see her (or him) as a cartoon. Learning anatomy is essential, and I want to take those body shapes and contours and reimagine the human form in a different way. I try to show the human figure like it is in motion and constantly moving.

I just finished reading a book on N. C. Wyeth; check out how dynamic his illustrations are. It feels like the characters are performing a movie in front of your eyes—and you can't create that fantasy without understanding the human body and how it moves.

I strongly encourage all artists to carry around a sketchbook or a piece of paper and a pen and to always be on the lookout for interesting people to draw.

After drawing all day at my animation board, sometimes it's great to relax and watch a movie; while watching the film, I'll be inspired to sketch one of the actors. There might be a certain gesture or way of seeing the actor's face that I never noticed before, and I think it could look really cool in my next film. So, under my coffee table at home, I have stacks of little sketches, tossed there in a blind fury after jotting down visual ideas.

CARICATURE OF A YOUNG JACK PALANCE FROM TV

Another talent that I believe is really undertaught in our schools is that of visual memory. This is the skill of seeing an image or a character, keeping it in your brain, then later putting it down on paper—I swear by this practice.

When I started my animation school in 2009, I would bring in a guest lecturer for about half an hour, and then, after the visiting artist had left, I'd ask the class to draw that person. The students hated me for it, but it really stressed the point that whenever we see something or someone, we should always be super observant. I call it a "brain camera." Study how something looks, search for the personality in everything—cars, clothes, buildings, toasters, and of course people. Because they all have a living soul, they all want to talk to you, and they all want to star in your next film. They won't ask for payment; they just want to be Hollywood stars, like everyone else. So get their images stuck in your brain. How would you portray them in pencil, colors, computer? What are their basic shapes and silhouettes, their essences? What kind of personalities would they have?

This is the fun part of animation—making life a game, having fun with life. Remember, there are no limits in animation. If making the film is not amusing for you, then something is wrong with the process. If it's not fun, find a way to make it fun, because if you're going to work on a film project for two years, you better damn well have a good time!

Caricatures

I spent 20 years as a professional caricature artist, but when I started out, I wasn't very good. I began when I was in the National Guard, and the captain knew I was an artist and that I hated doing military drills. So he put me in charge of creating drawings of all the officers— and I had to learn to draw portraits very fast, or I'd be kicked out onto the rifle range. Some of those drawings were very crude, but I had a strong incentive to improve.

I studied the caricatures of David Levine, Robert Grossman, and a college friend of mine, Bruce McGillivray. He's a brilliant caricaturist, and he was a huge influence on me, and I slowly learned the craft and got better.

Caricature is the essence of animation because you can take the human face and exaggerate it to the point of humor. Animation is basically the same process—exaggerating the essential parts of the character or movement and minimizing the rest.

I'm now going to give you a few pointers on how I create caricatures; at the same time, you'll

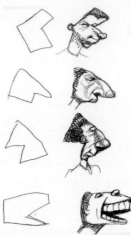

NEVER MAKE A CARICATURE USING AN OVAL. TRY TO FIND A SHAPE THAT IS UNIQUE AND COMPELLING, AND YOU'LL DEVELOP VERY INTERESTING CHARACTERS.

be learning how I create animation—the rules are very similar.

To start, look at the human face as a shape, a three-dimensional sphere, a ball of clay to be molded. Don't be concerned with hair or facial details. Concentrate only on the shape. All human heads are oval, but making an oval is very bland. You want to create an outline that's unique, dynamic, memorable. So play around with different shapes, looks, and styles.

Once you have a pleasing, exciting shape that generally represents your model, you're ready to move on to more detail. The next step is defining the facial features—the eyes, nose, mouth, and ears. Very roughly, put some simple lines to indicate where those features are placed—remember, you may want to move them around later, but it's important to get a rough idea of their relationships to each other.

Just as the human body should have a line of action (as Preston Blair calls it), so should the face. When I start to create a caricature, I either imagine or sketch a line of action in the face. This step is crucial for the success of the drawing because it's like a gesture for the face and it reveals the personality in a very simple form.

This line of action should be used in designing the layout of the shot. I use it constantly to control the viewer's eye and to show it where to look, and it makes the viewer so much more involved in the film.

I find that often the very first time I see someone's face is when the design is clearest. I don't know why that is; perhaps because it seems unique and different

(LEFT TO RIGHT) DEBORAH HARRY, DIANA ROSS, CARLY SIMON, DOLLY PARTON, LINDA RONSTADT FOR *VANITY FAIR*, UNPUBLISHED (1983)

YOUNG JACK ELAM

WOODY ALLEN

SOPHIA LOREN

TONY PERKINS

CARY GRANT

RONALD REAGAN

ELVIS PRESLEY

ALFRED HITCHCOCK

ROBERT DUVALL

YOUNG JOHN TRAVOLTA

HARRISON FORD

HUMPHREY BOGART

ROD STEWART

and then all of his or her characteristics are much more apparent. Likewise, the more I study a face, the harder it is to see the caricature's potential in it—the face becomes too familiar and commonplace. Every face can be reduced to its essence; all people and objects have an essence, and the purpose of caricature is to exaggerate that essence. That is what animation does: it shows you the essence of character and movement. Simplify!

If I'm doing a caricature and I've come to the point where I have no idea how a certain face is unique, I'll place it beside a group of other faces, and all of a sudden, it becomes clear how to exaggerate the features. Or, if the drawing is not going well, I'll often leave it alone for a day, put it up on the wall at a distance, and when I see it fresh, I'll know immediately what's wrong with the drawing.

Another trick is to look at the drawing's reflection in a mirror—sometimes the imperfections immediately make themselves known, and I'm able to fix them. It's a new and different view of the drawing, so it's like you're seeing it for the first time.

Another trick I use is to try and give a verbal description of the face—for example, his head was like a head of lettuce, or had the look of a claw hammer. Then I just draw those objects and add the features.

DESIGN—IN THIS ROUGH PENCIL SKETCH FROM *CHEATIN'* YOU CAN SEE HOW I PUSH THE EYE AROUND. JAKE'S BODY ARC CURVES AROUND THE LADY AND POINTS TO THE HEROINE (ELLA) IN THE FRONT CAR. ALSO, HIS HEAD IS KIND OF A POINTER THAT DRAWS YOUR ATTENTION TO ELLA AND THE BONNET.

Another interesting aspect about caricature is that there are so many different ways to draw one subject's face, and they can all be correct—there is never only one unique way to draw someone. When I used to hang out with a lot of caricature artists, I was amazed by how many variations of Ronald Reagan or George Bush's face there could be, and they all seemed perfect.

When I had my school of animation, I had one session that was strictly for caricature—I had the class draw me, first very handsome and flattering, and then in a second drawing with more of an ugly and evil interpretation. This is a talent that is incredibly important in animation, because when you're trying to create emotions and personality, you must get very theatrical. You have to know all the extremes of a personality, and how to express them. We all have the potential for good and evil in us, and as artists, we have to be able to show the entire spectrum.

The Human Body

When I look at the portfolios of young artists, the same bad habits keep popping up. These ugly

THIS IS A CARICATURE OF YOURS TRULY—FIRST AS A COMPLIMENTARY STUDY AND THEN AS AN INSULTING PORTRAIT.

drawings could have easily been improved by taking some life-drawing classes or by the study of great art.

Unfortunately, the only art these students have looked at is animé—and thus all of their drawings have the same look and feel. People with big eyes, and giant robot monsters—please, students, don't use this stuff in your portfolio! It's great that animé inspired you to become an animator, but widen your horizons. One of the reasons I quit teaching is that I had a bellyful of Japanese manga art.

I highly encourage young artists to widen their perspectives and to go to museums, galleries, and bookstores to look at other styles of art. See a lot of animation, not just Disney and animé, but also Warner Bros., the Fleischer brothers, indie animation, Russian, British, French—there are so many beautiful styles and visual ideas out there to influence you. Why stick to one boring genre?

I will list all the difficult parts of the human body that students and professionals have trouble drawing—and how to fix those drawings. First, the feet—as I've said earlier, why do young artists insist on drawing huge, cartoonish shoes? Haven't we progressed enough to be able to draw decent shoes?

I realize that shoes and feet are hard to draw, but it's important to not use old, outdated designs. Look at your own feet and shoes—draw them, over and over and over, and then you'll feel comfortable drawing great feet. Look at the great shoes drawn by Winsor McCay or A. B. Frost.

Clothing is another weak spot, not only for young artists but also for professionals. Look at the multi-million-dollar Pixar and DreamWorks films—the great computers have still not been able to recreate the look of real fabric. It looks like all the characters are wearing rubber suits—it's so artificial! With all the money going into these films, can't they design a program to simulate fabric folds?

Loose clothing is one of my favorite subjects to draw. Sometimes I get all caught up in the folds and bends of a loose pair of pants. One of the things I hate about

Notice how all the dark shadowed fabrice folds point to stress points in the character.

hands

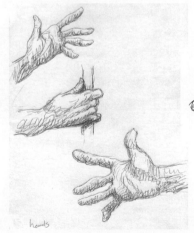

hands

life-drawing classes is that they rarely have models wearing loose clothes. That would be a thing of beauty for me, an otherwise nude model wearing a pair of loose trousers!

There's a gorgeous pattern of design in fabric, and once you figure out how it works, you become a much freer artist, in that you can draw anything. And that makes it feel like you're flying: there are no limits!

When drawing a person with loose clothing, be sure to be aware of the stress points. These are parts of the body with sharp angles, and you'll notice how all of the wrinkles point to these extreme angles, but in concert with the pointing of the angles, also be aware of the pull of gravity. These two forces working together create a beautiful apparel design. Check out the work of the great Will Eisner for his fabric design.

The hands, for me, are still the most difficult subjects to draw. There are hundreds of bones in the hand; thus there are hundreds of different positions that the hand can form. Consequently, the hands' different shapes are limitless, and that makes it a tough model.

One of the issues that really bugs me is when young artists make the hands gigantic—that's the first tip-off that they're amateurs. I can't tell you how many times I've seen huge hands in a beginner's artwork. Why do they do that? You'd think that since they can't draw hands well, they'd prefer to make them small and hide them. Well, I wish they would. When I was a young artist, I went through this phase myself, but fortunately I didn't spend much time there.

Try to find a style for the hands that gives them the proper look and feel, yet is your own style. Study the great hands drawn by other artists—the works of A. B. Frost and Winsor McCay are a good place to start.

ONE OF MY ONLY DRAWINGS TO USE LARGE HANDS

Of course, you can always use your own hand as a model. It's always available for model work, cheap. The more you draw hands, the more you'll develop a great animated hand.

NOTICE HOW ALL THE BONES—LEGS, FEET, ARMS, FINGERS—FACE INWARD EXCEPT FOR THE THUMBS. ALSO NOTICE HOW THE WRINKLES ALL POINT TO THE STRESS POINTS.

Here's another animating tip: every bone in the human body turns inward, so when you're drawing the human body walking, or jumping, or in action, it looks really cool to exaggerate the bones as they all turn inward. My theory is that when we're in the womb, we're scrunched up in a little ball in order to not poke our extremities into our mothers' stomachs and that smooth ball makes delivery that much easier.

However, there is one bone that doesn't follow this rule, for some reason, and that's the thumb. The thumb is the only bone that bends outward, rather than inward. It's odd—what does that mean?

The Face

We've now come to the face—the most fascinating of subjects. I could do a whole film on the face. In fact, I did; it's called "Your Face."

To me, it's the ultimate cliché: when we're born, our mother's face is the first thing we see. Our face is our identity; it's the image on our passport. There is so much emotion and personality that can be communicated by just a small movement of the eyebrow, an adjustment of the eye, or a quiver of the chin.

A. B. Frost, or Peter Chung—just a few simple scribbles and you can draw very cool, interesting eyes.

A lot of young artists also like to draw huge noses, perhaps thinking that the larger the nose, the funnier the character is. Unfortunately, the larger the nose is, the harder it is to give that character a three-dimensional personality. The nose gets in the way of any subtlety or depth in the being.

That's why it's obligatory to learn how to draw the face. But the human face is the hardest subject to draw. I can look at a student's portraits and I can immediately see whether they have artistic talent.

Here are some tricks of drawing the face that I've learned over the years.

Please don't make big saucer eyes! In fact, eyes are much more engaging if they are simple, small shapes. Look at the eyes drawn by Winsor McCay,

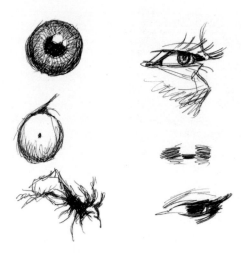

RANDOM EYES

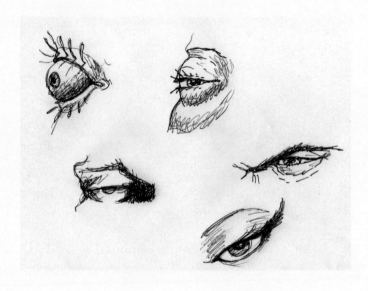

NOTICE HOW NOSE AND MOUTH SHADOWS GIVE THE FACE A SENSE OF REALITY.

Only rarely do I use exaggerated noses, and I do that with the utmost of care. For me, the best way to draw a nose is by use of the shadow. It's a better indication of where the nose is. There is a big difference between the genders with regard to noses, and I do take advantage of that.

And here's a trick for drawing the mouth. The lips, like the eyes, are on a curved surface, so use that to give dimension to the mouth. Beginners always forget to show the famous "lip ledge"—I don't know why they do that, but they are missing a great opportunity. The size of the lip ledge indicates the sexiness of the mouth—I use it all the time.

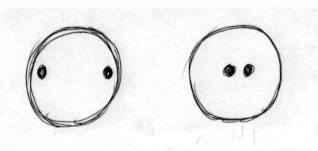

(FIRST PICTURE) A BABY'S EYES POSITION (SECOND PICTURE) AN OLDER PERSON'S EYES POSITION

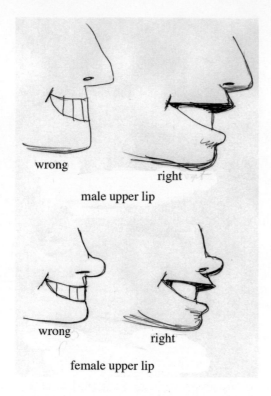

wrong

right

male upper lip

wrong

right

female upper lip

And utilize the dark areas at the end of the teeth; they help define the curvature of the teeth.

Another cool trick is to exaggerate the cheeks and the jaw as someone is screaming or laughing. The jaw never just goes lower, it actually butts up against the neck and creates a cool triangle shape with the cheeks. Again, look for dynamic triangular shapes when drawing the face—they're much more compelling and interesting.

A lot of Disney's classic animated films have around eight or ten mouth positions for lip-synching to dialogue, but I've found that you can make all the words in the English language with just four mouth positions.

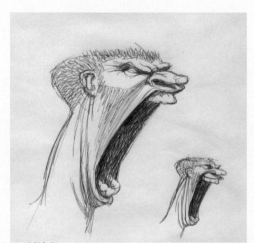

THIS IS A CLASSIC EXPRESSION THAT IS USED FOR MANY FACIAL
EMOTIONS. THE YELL, THE YAWN—IT'S ALSO VERY CLOSE TO A FEARFUL
SCREAM, AND A LAUGH. NOTICE HOW THE LOWER JAW ROTATES DOWN
AGAINST THE NECK, AND ALSO HOW THE TOP OF THE HEAD FROM TEETH UP
COMPRESSES TO A QUARTER THE LENGTH OF THE HEAD.

FACIAL PERSPECTIVES: IT'S A LOT OF FUN TO USE FORCED PERSPECTIVE
WITH FACES, WHICH GIVES THE HEAD A MUCH MORE POWERFUL AND
INTENSE LOOK.

DIFFERENT NOSES

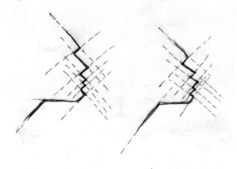

NOTICE IN THESE HEAD PROFILES HOW YOU CAN USE THE PARALLEL LINES
TO CONSTRUCT A SILHOUETTE.

WHEN YOU'RE MAKING LIFE DRAWINGS, EXPERIMENT WITH ODD AND UNUSUAL ANGLES OF THE BODY AND FACE. THESE COME IN HANDY IN THE ANIMATION PROCESS.

USE THE FACE AS A POINTER TO DIRECT OUR ATTENTION.

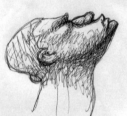

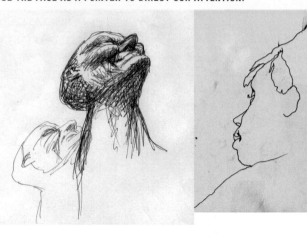

If you get a chance, check out my short film "The Wiseman," which also appeared in my feature film *The Tune*. When the Wiseman talks, and he says a lot, I used only four drawings, for about two minutes of animation—now that's a shortcut! But no one was bothered that I used only four drawings for that long, because it worked.

"THE WISEMAN" (1992)

Also, never draw the face as a balanced sketch—that's death to a drawing. It's always more compelling if it's uneven, unbalanced, or distorted. Look at the great caricatures of Philip Burke; his faces are so off-center that they become puzzles that suck your eye

deeper into the art. You can't take your eye away from that face, and that's the way it should be.

Drawing the female face is a minefield full of traps. But if you follow a few simple rules, she'll look beautiful: large hair; eyes wide apart (not necessarily large); big, vertical lips (not horizontal); high cheekbones; long, thin neck; big eyelashes; and a nose that's small and close to the upper lip.

It's my own theory that the basic shape of the human head is horizontal. I occasionally do vertical heads but more as a cartoon shape. I feel that the character is so much stronger with a flatter head shape. Also, it facilitates the pointing aspect of the design.

and how they see it. To me, the face is the perfect tool to help control the viewer's eye, and I use it incessantly.

Design

When drawing props and inanimate objects, you must think of them as animate objects, as if they're alive, they have personality, they have souls. Otherwise, these items will be very boring to look at. For example, I've seen a lot of guns drawn like this:

FACES AND BODIES ALWAYS LOOK MORE INTERESTING WHEN THEY ARE OFF BALANCE AND ASKEW. SYMMETRY IS VERY BORING; IT'S A MARK OF AN AMATEUR.

My final tip is to use the face as a design ingredient. I can't stress enough how important it is to push the viewer's eye around the screen. Use the drawings as directional signals to control what the audience sees

But for me, this is a sissy gun. A gun is masculine, it's macho—it's got muscles. It's not a delicate piece of ornamentation. No, it's a brutal, powerful statement—so try drawing your pistols like they are characters in your story.

And that brings us to our next category in animation: design.

To me, it's the arrangement of shapes so that they form a powerful image that is used to meet the creator's needs. For example, if I want to create a feeling of peace and beauty, I'll arrange shapes in such a way as to meet those ends. I'll use soft, complimentary colors and shapes that have an easy flow. Or perhaps I want to communicate a feeling of violence, so the design might be much more aggressive or shocking, with bright colors and hard edges.

I can't tell you how important design is to a great film. Again, look at some of N. C. Wyeth's wonderful illustrations to see examples of how he used great design to push the eye around and to make you look where he wants you to look in order to capture your imagination and boost the powerful human emotions in the visuals. He used very little detail, and the detail he used was only to draw the eye to certain areas. The rest of the painting was dark shapes that have almost an abstract feel.

And that's where design comes in. Here is a drawings in which I manipulate the eyeballs of the audience.

USE PERSPECTIVE TO PUSH THE EYE. JUST TRY TO LOOK AWAY FROM THE GUY'S HEAD—IT'S VERY DIFFICULT. MANY PICTORIAL ELEMENTS CAN BE USED TO DIVERT THE EYE.

Silhouettes

One way to control the eyes is to use silhouettes. I use silhouettes a lot, especially in my later films. They allow me to heighten the drama of any scene; they also make it quicker to draw. If you watch a lot of film noir, you'll see how effective and powerful silhouettes can be.

Another variation of the silhouette is the use of soft focus or depth-of-field visuals. In this technique, you draw the eye to a certain part of the frame by putting everything else out of focus (or making everything else silhouetted). I have been using this technique increasingly often because it's such a great, visual way to tell a story.

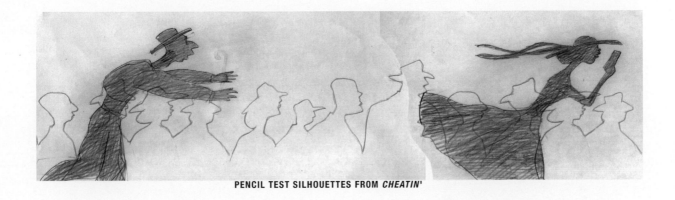

PENCIL TEST SILHOUETTES FROM *CHEATIN'*

Many of the early motion pictures had a lush feel because they had that shallow depth of field and everything on the edges of the frame was blurry. I want to bring that look back because it lends itself so well to animated fantasy films.

Previz

Every morning before I attack the drawing board for a ten-hour animation session, I like to lie in bed and visualize all the scenes I'll be drawing that day. Usually, I can draw about four or five shots a day, so I lay there and roll the images around in my mind (today, they call it "previz" for previsualization). It seems like the more I lie there, imagining each shot, the better the shots get. I mentally play with the backgrounds and try different looks; I play with the perspectives, the timing, the camera angles, and the shadows, always trying to make them better, clearer, funnier, and/or more appealing.

After about an hour or so of this, I know each shot very intimately—every detail is solid and clear in my head. Then I rush to my drawing board and copy the drawings from my memory to the paper. This stage is the reason that the retention of imagery is such a valuable talent. So I sit at my drawing board, not wanting to lose those precious images, and I whip up the animation as fast as I can—sometimes very

ASSORTED WALKING POSTURES

roughly so that I capture the essence before I forget. I become so obsessed with the art that I often forget to go to the office.

Or, if the shot is particularly extravagant or complex, I'll draw little thumbnail storyboards so that I can refer to them throughout the day, but this routine of visualizing the day's artwork is very connected to my childhood love of daydreaming, so I guess I'm still a child, daydreaming my feature film.

Walk Cycles

Every animator has to know how to create walk cycles. They're one of the most basic skills of any animator. They're also fun to do.

I'll give you my basic walk cycles, plus some extras, using different perspectives.

If you want to see great books on walking cycles, check out either the Preston Blair classic, *Animation*, or the great Richard Williams book *The Animator's Survival Kit*.

A WOMAN WALKING, REAR VIEW

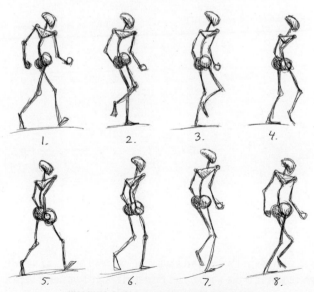

WALKING CYCLE, ¾ VIEW FROM THE BACK

RUNNING, SIDE VIEW

THIS IS ANOTHER TRICK I USE TO SAVE TIME. INSTEAD OF THE 11 NORMAL STEPS TO WALK TO THE HOUSE, I DO IT IN 5 STEPS. IT'S SO MUCH EASIER, AND IT ACTUALLY LOOKS A LOT COOLER.

Point of View

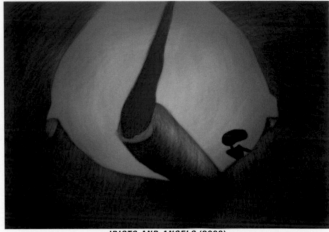

IDIOTS AND ANGELS (2008)

It's amazing how many people don't know my name when I introduce myself, but immediately recognize my work if they see it. I like that! My style has become quite identifiable.

I've carved out a niche—albeit a weird niche—in the pantheon of animation; it's called branding. In other words, I'm like the Jim Jarmusch or the John Waters of animation, which I don't particularly mind.

One of the reasons for this identity, aside from my pencil technique, is my use of a weird *point of view* (POV). I love to play with visuals; I'm always looking for different ways to visually tell a story. To me, that's what makes animation so much fun: finding inventive and creative ways to imagine the everyday world. It's too boring and too bland otherwise.

I like to take normal storytelling devices and kick them in the ass. I want to put the camera in places it's never been before. And that's what's great about animation: there are no limits, no strict visual rules. I want to show you things that no one else has seen before. Also, I believe that the audience wants to see the world differently, too, so I'm always looking for fresh, bizarre camera angles.

In *Idiots and Angels,* I have a real fun shot of a dance scene, but the shot is from the inside of an ashtray (everyone in the film smokes), so the first thing you see is a large lit end of a cigarette with smoke billowing from it. Then, far off in the distance, you can see the couple dancing by. A lot of people have mentioned that shot as being very weird—I love it!

I love using an interesting POV. I've done a number of films using this kind of POV, including "One of Those Days," "The Exciting Life of a Tree," and one

of my favorites, "Draw!", in which we see the world in slow motion from the point of view of a bullet being fired out of a gun to kill a cowboy. It's so interesting to play around with POV.

I believe that life is enriched by seeing the world from different angles. Everyone has many sides to their personalities. Hitler was a vegetarian—he loved animals and didn't want to harm them—that's a side of him I find fascinating. So that's why I love seeing stories from different angles and unique viewpoints. Try it in your film; see how many bizarre places you can put the camera.

I often like to play a visual game when I'm flying across the country. From 20,000 feet up, I'll see a car speeding down a freeway and imagine what the driver is seeing when he looks up at me in my airplane: how do I look? And perhaps he then looks at a hitchhiker on the side of the road, and I magically fly into the hiker's head to see his vision of the car and the plane. Then perhaps I zap into a cactus in the desert nearby, how it would view the hitchhiker, and so on. I find these games fun and visually stimulating, and often I get good ideas from playing bizarre games like this. That's how boring my life is.

POV OF BULLET IN *DRAW!* (1993)

Perspective and Foreshortening

Another trick I use to capture the eyeballs of the viewer is playing around with *perspective* and *foreshortening*, which means exaggerating the size of certain objects to give the illusion of depth. In other words, if a guy is pointing a gun at the camera, the gun would be extremely large (super close up) and the man's face would be very small by comparison.

This look can also be achieved by using a wide-angle or "fish-eye" lens. These lenses are often used for dramatic effect or to show that a character is on some kind of drug trip. However, I like to use the exaggerated perspective all the time—it makes the viewers feel like they're in a dream, a fantastic place. For me, it heightens the intensity and makes the visuals much more memorable.

In association with exaggerated foreshortening, I like to play with the vanishing point perspective. In high school art classes, learning proper perspective is one of the foundations, but I like to screw around with it.

In college, I saw the famous *Mystery and Melancholy of a Street* by Giorgio de Chirico. I thought, "Wow, this guy really needs to take lessons in perspective." Yet the painting was such a jumble of different vanishing points that it stuck in my head. It really was a haunted mystery. And then I understood it, and thought, "Wow, I should play around with skewed perspectives in my films and see what happens." And it just happened that it fit in quite well with my weird camera angles and distorted foreshortening.

DESIGN IDEAS TO MAKE YOUR LAYOUTS MORE INTERESTING. (THANKS TO "WALLY WOOD'S 22 PANELS THAT ALWAYS WORK.")

Distortion

The third trick I use for my Plympton style is *distortion*—playing with the imagery. Of course, the first and best example of this I used was in the short film "Your Face," and that film was such a big success that I've used the technique in almost all of my films.

Distortion is actually a very close cousin to exaggeration; however, I like to use distortion more as a visual tool to tell a story, not so much as a comedic tool. Often the distortion can be quite subtle, and sometimes not. In my film "Push Comes to Shove," I have an excellent example of extreme distortion: one of the gentlemen places a mouse, cat, and dog inside the other man's mouth, and naturally the animals begin to fight with each other, causing the man's head to take on extremely weird shapes. This distortion goes on for quite a while, so it was a real pleasure for me to draw. It was as if I had taken a plateful of psychedelic drugs.

Around that time, I learned another important lesson; this one may seem obvious to you, but to me

"PUSH COMES TO SHOVE" (1990)

it was a real breakthrough. I was trying to draw a giant, and I thought, "Well, he's a giant, so I have to make everything big!" So I made all of his features larger than normal—big feet, big hands, big head, big shoulders, big legs, everything. But when I finished the drawing, he looked exactly like he did before, only he filled the frame, so there was no more room for the other characters!

That's when it struck me: sometimes it's easier to create largeness by just shrinking the other parts of the art. Ah, but what parts to shrink? Once I shrunk his hands, feet, and head, he suddenly looked like a real giant. So remember: sometimes shrinking some features makes other objects look bigger.

Shadows

Another distinctive quality of my films is the use of shadows. It really bugs me how the Disney films of the 1980s and 1990s were so expensive—budgets of hundreds of millions of dollars—yet they refused to use shadows, whereas the Miyazaki films have this gorgeous use of shadows with a budget that's a fraction of that of the Disney films.

Why do the Disney films not make good use of shadows? Shadows add color and dimension to the characters—they make them look so real and lifelike. I believe that the wonderful shadows you find in the Miyazaki films are one of the main reasons they are so well-loved.

SHADOWS ARE ONE OF THE MOST IMPORTANT PARTS OF VISUAL STORYTELLING. THEY HELP DEFINE THE VOLUME AND THREE DIMENSIONS OF ANY PIECE OF ART. THEY ADD A SENSE OF REALITY TO ANY CARTOON, NO MATTER HOW BASIC OR CRUDE. SOMETIMES I LIKE TO CREATE CHARACTERS USING ONLY SHADOWS AND NO LINES. TRY IT! IT'S FUN.

At a fairly early age—I think I was in basic training at Fort Ord, where the sun shined every day and created wonderfully colorful shadows—I became obsessed with shadows. Not just those projected on the ground, but also on people's clothing and faces.

I became so obsessed that I started creating drawings using just shadows. No lines, no textures, nothing but shadows. It's a great exercise; it teaches you how to look at a visual image in a completely fresh way. Shadows add bulk and solidity to a drawing. You can feel that a character's persona is much more real—it has weight. I'd love to do a film in which everything is defined by shadows.

Falling man

And the ever-present shadow on the ground gives them an integration into the background—you feel that they are much more connected to the picture. I also love using shadows on the wall to add drama, mystery, and variety to the story. Look at the wonderful Orson Welles film *Citizen Kane* and see how he uses shadows not just on the body, but projected on the walls and ground. Another great shadow film to check out is *The Third Man*, a very fantasy-oriented noir film.

Experiment with shadows; they are so much fun to play with, and they create such great visuals.

Metamorphosis

If you saw my Oscar-nominated film "Your Face," then you're aware of another popular trick I use very often: *metamorphosis*. I don't claim to have invented it; if you look at the very first animated shorts, "Fantasmagorie" (1908) by the Frenchman Émile Cohl or "Humorous Phases of Funny Faces" (1906) by James Stuart Blackton, you'll discover that metamorphosis was the very foundation of the charm of the earliest animated films. But along the way, Walt Disney emphasized a more realistic type of storytelling. Well, I decided to bring magical transformations back.

One of the more popular parts of *Idiots and Angels* is when the Angel character gets up in the morning and the shower becomes the faucet, then the milk in the cereal. Then the spoon in his mouth transforms into a key in his car's ignition. It seemed like a fun and original way to get the character off to work.

Animation is the perfect art form for metamorphosis. Try it; you'll like it.

Pencil Test

In the big, wide world of corporate animation, everyone has his or her specific job: lighting, effects, key animation, or whatever. There seem to be a thousand different specialty occupations.

But when you're an independent filmmaker like me, you have to do all that stuff by yourself. There are no in-betweeners, no clean-up people, no breakdown artists. I do it all. Why? Because I'm too cheap, and also because it's fun. I feel more in control when I can fully design the characters to my desires and then make them come to life.

Therefore, I rarely shoot my drawings on ones, meaning 24 drawings per second (one for each frame of film). Quite frankly, I don't believe the average viewer can tell the difference, or even cares, whether animation is shot on ones or twos (one drawing for every two frames of film).

I even consider one drawing for every three frames of film appropriate for me—it feels smooth enough. And if I'm really feeling bold, I'll shoot on fours or fives. Sure, the movement is a little jerky, but often that's appropriate for the action. In fact, my films can never compete with Disney films—I can't match their budgets and professionalism. If their films are like hundred-piece orchestras, my films are more like garage bands—raw, crude, and sometimes offensive. And I like it that way. My audience is definitely a lot younger and more rebellious, though I haven't seen a mosh pit at any of my screenings.

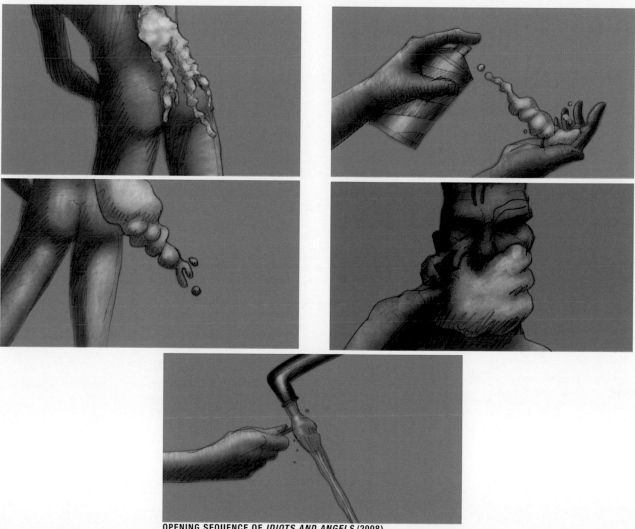

OPENING SEQUENCE OF *IDIOTS AND ANGELS* (2008),
SHOWING METAMORPHOSIS

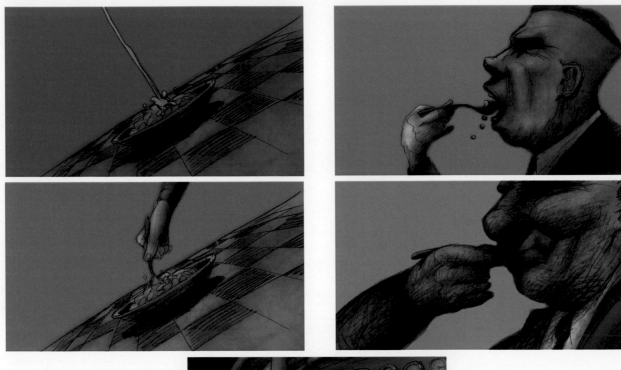

OPENING SEQUENCE OF *IDIOTS AND ANGELS* (2008), SHOWING METAMORPHOSIS

Having said that, you'll see that my exposure sheets (charts indicating which drawing goes in which frame of film) are very loose. I try to maintain a close relationship with the person scanning my drawings, and often I'll make many adjustments to the timing once the pencil test is finished, at which point I can retime the drawings to my imagination.

Viewing the pencil test many times really helps me get the timing correct. In fact, I believe that showing the pencil test to a number of people—and getting feedback from them—is essential.

I often do shows at festivals and schools, where I show my works in progress, so I'm forced to watch the rough pencil tests with an audience, sometimes with a temporary soundtrack, which really helps me see what needs to be fixed.

The students often make comments or suggestions that help me improve the film. But more often, by just watching the film in an audience situation I can intuitively tell what's wrong with the picture. And the more I watch it, the better the corrections are.

A SAMPLE EXPOSURE SHEET. VERY SIMPLE, I KNOW, BUT IT MEETS MY NEEDS.

I get this question a lot—and I know most animation these days is done using breakdown artists, in-betweeners and such, but I like to create all of my own drawings.

There are a number of reasons why I create all of my own animation art. When I was making *Hair High,* I thought I might use some other animators to help me speed up the process. They did wonderful work, but I constantly had to redraw their shots because they didn't follow the image I had in my head—and how could they? The other animators couldn't see inside my brain. There's no window in my skull.

Because I had to constantly adjust their drawings, it actually slowed down the production and didn't really help that much. And on top of all that, it was very expensive. So that's why I stopped hiring other artists to help with the animation.

Once I've revised the pencil test to the point where it meets my expectations, and those of my friends, I'm ready to finish the film. I go through all of the artwork again, fixing any rough spots, accenting the outlines, adding texture and tone to the artwork, and going in with my eraser to bring out the highlights. I make some last-minute touches such as bringing out the details, especially in faces, and blurring areas that aren't important—again, in order to direct the eyes to the areas I want them to see.

Backgrounds

Because I started out as an illustrator, as you can imagine, I'm a big fan of backgrounds. They are a very important ingredient in the success of a film. But because I usually create my own backgrounds, I like to stay away from artwork that has too much detail. I don't want the backdrop to compete with the action in the foreground.

Again, this is my "pushing the eye" theory; if the viewer's eyeball gets caught up in the minutiae of the artwork behind the action, I'm in big trouble. I want the eye to get involved in the story, not the art.

The background should enhance the storytelling and perhaps bring an ambience or flavor to the location, and nothing else. If it does get too rich in detail, I may have to soften the focus a bit to make sure the characters are clearly observed. I want the characters to "read."

If the characters are not in view and the background is a location shot or has some information that's essential to the story, then by all means, I go crazy with detail. But remember, I want to push the eye to that feature in the background that's essential to the plot.

OPENING BACKGROUND FROM *IDIOTS AND ANGELS* (2008)

Perfectionism

I get a lot of criticism about my films. People say that they're too raw and unfinished and that they have too many imperfections. And you know what? They're right: my films are jam-packed full of mistakes. Booboos abound, problems aplenty.

But that's okay! I don't want to make perfect films—perfect films are anathema to me. It's like having a perfect lover: their hair is always in place, there are no wrinkles on their clothes, they never make mistakes, and they have no faults. Would you want to live with someone like that?

I want someone who's human—whose frailties and foibles are endearing. That's what makes love happen.

"Perfect is boring."

—TINA FEY

An old girlfriend once told me that she liked someone for their charms but she loved him for his weaknesses. Well, that's how I feel about my films.

They each have a personality, a style, and an identity, and my crudeness and edginess are parts of my style.

I know this one animator who made a film that many people called the greatest film ever made! It constantly ranks as the most "perfect" animated short ever. God, what a millstone that is! Now he's working on his follow-up film. But how can he finish it, when it has to be better than the greatest film ever made? He's been working on this follow-up film for 20 years, and he's frozen by perfection. Twenty years to make a short film; how does he live during all that time? I have no idea.

For me, mistakes are cool. They can often lead to great ideas and new directions. I'll be walking down the crowded streets of New York and overhear a conversation, and because the surrounding noise level is so loud, I don't always hear the words clearly. I misunderstand the words, and my brain makes up something completely different. That's what I mean when I say mistakes can lead to great creativity.

And that's where a lot of my ideas come from: mistakes and misperceptions. Sometimes the absurdity of these errors is a perfect source for many of my ideas. And it's not just misheard conversations. If I take my glasses off, I'll see things that are not in fact part of reality—mistakes again. Sometimes I purposely hinder my senses so I can make a lot of misunderstandings, and I get a lot of ideas that way. Often these crazy ideas are a great source of visual jokes.

But I also value mistakes in my art. I like to animate quickly; that way, a lot of options open up in terms of design. The looser the drawing, the more creative I become. These very rough drawings—more like sketches—are actually very impressionistic and much more compelling to look at.

It's kind of like going to a museum and marveling at the hand-drawn art. You can feel the hand of the artist. But with a computer-made film, it feels more like watching a machine. The artwork is cold and impersonal, and perfect. I prefer the warmer, mistake-filled, handmade, funky feel of my artwork over a cold piece of perfection made by a computer. I've got my own proprietary software; it's called a "pencil."

A side effect to being a perfectionist is thinking you're the greatest artist in the world. I've seen many filmmakers crash and burn because of their ego, vanity, and hubris. Please have a little humility. We're competing against each other, and that's what makes us better, but appreciate other people's films. No one's perfect; we're all trying to make a living in animation, and there's no room for self-indulgent narcissists.

In fact, it's very dangerous once you have a big hit. You win lots of prizes and believe you have the magic formula for success. You don't! Audiences change; they're fickle. What's funny one year could be pathetic the next. The audience is like a mutating virus—they always want something different.

That's why I'm always experimenting with new drawing styles, new techniques, and new kinds of stories. My career would be very boring if I kept making the same film over and over. I think that's the reason I never got into a TV series.

Color

It's very disturbing to me when I get young animators visiting me in my studio to show me their animated films that make absolutely offensive use of color in their films—I often react in horror. It's gotten so bad that I have to wear sunglasses to look at students' work.

Don't they teach color theory any more in school? How hard can it be to show the students the proper use of color? How can you be an artist of any kind and not appreciate the power of the palette?

Color is like a very fast car: it can be very dangerous if not handled properly. Artists should have a license to use color. Young artists should start with the easy colors—earth tones and pastels. Then, once they feel comfortable, they can move up to higher speeds with brighter, faster colors.

I don't have the time or space in this book to give you a complete tutorial on color theory. However, I can give you a few pointers on how to use colors in your film.

Color is extremely powerful. If used properly, it can create magic. If not, you will crash and burn. I don't care how beautiful your drawings are or how good the story is—badly used color will sabotage the entire project. I hate to be repetitive, but I like to use color to push the eye around. Color can be like highway signs, telling people where to look and how to look.

RANDOM SKETCH (1971)

Everyone knows that the right color can set the mood—that's important for engaging people into the story, whether it's a war story, a romance, a comedy, or a pastoral. The color sets the mood that carries you along on the magical trip.

- If it's a battle scene, you want lots of intense, hot colors: reds, yellows, and blacks.
- Romance colors are more along the lines of soft blues and gauzy pinks or pastels.
- Comedy usually involves basic, brighter colors.
- Pastoral moods bring in soft greens and browns.

I remember one student who came in and showed me his short suburban comedy, and for some reason, a tree far in the background was colored bright lime green. Now, I don't remember what happened on that

AUTUMN SCENE FROM *HAIR HIGH* (2004)

street, what the people said, or where they went. The only object I was concerned about was that damn lime green tree! What the hell? Why didn't his teacher tell him to change that color?

I believe what happened was this: he was playing with his computer's color wheel and just thought that his trees should be this beautiful, bright green color because it was a comedy. He never thought about that color in relation to the other colors.

That's the secret: all of the hues have to be balanced throughout every image. And it's that balance that determines the effectiveness of the palette. It's the same as with the instruments in an orchestra, which all have to work together to direct the attention of the listener to specific and emotional areas of the composition.

I like to keep the intensity of color dialed way down. I like the "noir" look. If you've seen *Idiots and Angels,* remember that the color is very minimal throughout the film, and only on the last image— the exterior of the house and the happy ending— do I bring out the color. And with *Hair High,* which takes place in a high school in the 1950s, I created a palette of soft pastels and used the bright hues only in the action scenes or very emotional sequences.

Bright colors such as lime green, crimson red, or electric purple should be labeled "handle with care," whereas wonderful tones such as earthy browns, manila, sepia, and grays are colors I use a lot. I call them "dead colors" because they are passive and don't intrude on my drawings.

However, when I was designing the color palette for "The Cow Who Wanted to Be a Hamburger," the story dictated bright primary colors because it's like a children's story, and I wanted the feel of a children's book—the kind of colors a child would use when coloring with crayons.

One day, while strolling though the Guggenheim Museum, I saw some of Wassily Kandinsky's early paintings. They were somewhat realistic (in fact, he did children's books in the early years of his career to support himself), and he employed the use of extremely bright, saturated hues. But he balanced them with large areas of black and white. I thought, "Wow! What a powerful mixture!"

So, when I drew the cow, I increased the size of the black shadows—in fact, sometimes the cow is a complete silhouette, with just a sliver of bright color along her face and back. Then I would add a bright white cloud on the sky, and the colors would practically sing. Bright palettes can be very useful; you just have to use them as part of the storytelling process.

Another trick is to not overuse blue for the sky. Often other colors will be more powerful and emotional as sky colors—pink, yellow, purple, grey— almost any color but blue.

Go to museums and check out the great usage of color in the impressionists' paintings—they seemed to really understand how to create moods with color. Also, look for a wonderful book by Leslie Cabarga, *The Designer's Guide to Color Combinations*—it's got everything you need to know about color patterns and theory.

COLOR ART FROM "THE COW WHO WANTED TO BE A HAMBURGER" (2010)

After I've finished all the art, I put the drawings in a manila folder along with the exposure sheets, backgrounds, and layouts, with instructions for camera moves—zooms, pans, and so on—and the film moves on to a process we call post-Bill production. I pass the project on to Desirée Stavracos, my project producer. She will now take over the text to explain what's involved in the digital process. Take it away, Desirée!

DESIRÉE STAVRACOS, BY BILL PLYMPTON

Digitizing the Art

As Bill mentioned earlier, it's my responsibility to oversee the scanning, cleaning, and compositing of his animation. Here's a breakdown on how his animation comes to life in the digital end of the production process.

Scanning

From the start of his animation career until 2004, Bill was shooting his animation on film. Even when the scanner was introduced to the animation industry (late 1980s, early 1990s), the cost of transferring from digital to film was such that scanning animation wasn't cost effective, even when weighed against the cost of developing film. By 2004, however, the scale had shifted, and scanning animation became the faster, cheaper method of bringing his drawings to the screen.

We scan all of Bill's drawings on flatbed scanners that import into Adobe Photoshop. Using a custom computer script that Adobe refers to as an "Action," we are able to automate the scanning and importing of the drawings so that they stack into single Photoshop files, which in turn represent individual sequences of animation (each layer in the Photoshop file is a drawing in the sequence). Once the various levels of animation and the background are scanned and organized into a scene folder, we move onto cleaning.

A NOTE FROM BILL

Let me chime in at this point. The use of digital scanning has freed me from using the bulky, crude, transparent cels and giant Rostrum camera. With the use of high-resolution scanners, the subtlety and depth of my pencil drawings comes through very clearly, especially on the giant movie screen. I believe it's one of the reasons *Idiots and Angels* was such a big success and *Hair High* was not.

Cleaning

What we call the cleaning process differs from film to film, depending on what media Bill chooses for a particular project. Generally, the cleaning process is twofold:

- **Part 1: dust and debris.** When scanning in animation, dust and other debris (eraser shavings, to be sure) usually find themselves between the drawing and the scanner bed, creating speckles or dots throughout the scenes. These have to be edited out before putting together finished scenes.
- **Part 2: cut-out.** Whereas in the past (when shooting on film), cels were employed so that animation laid seamlessly on a background, today we digitally "cut out" the animation. At this point, if Bill hasn't added color using his signature colored-pencil style, then we do it digitally.

Color

When done digitally, the coloring process is also completed in Photoshop. Bill will work out a palette with our production team, giving us reference and walking us through the style of the project and mood of the scene. The color is placed on a layer underneath the drawing layer, and the first pass is always flat color. For projects such as "The Cow Who Wanted to Be a Hamburger," the color stays flat. For films such as *Idiots and Angels*, however, we use digital brushes to apply shading and texture to the colored areas. By using the "dodge" and "burn" tools in conjunction with one of Photoshop's many preloaded textured brushes, we are able to sculpt the forms, helping strengthen the highlights and shadows that Bill builds with his many passes with the pencil.

Whichever method we use for applying color, our next step is to sequence our now-finished drawings and place them on top of the background in a process we call *compositing*.

Compositing

We put Bill's scenes together using another Adobe product, After Effects. After Effects allows us to import the layered Photoshop files and sequence them in a few short steps. We can also change timing from ones, twos, and threes on the fly, therefore creating previews and pencil tests faster than ever.

We also use After Effects to generate all of our camera moves, as well as special effects. With every iteration of After Effects, the modular control of motion from key frame to key frame (commonly known as

MY ANIMATED PENCIL DRAWINGS FROM *IDIOTS AND ANGELS* (2008)

THE COLORED VERSION OF THE SAME DRAWING; NOTICE THE DEPTH AND THE CHIAROSCURO IN THE COLORED VERSION.

tweening) is increasingly refined, allowing us to create digital solutions for what would normally be very challenging to animate in a traditional fashion. Also, After Effects' stock collection of plug-ins helps us to create convincing lighting effects, blurs, and camera shakes.

Finally, we use After Effects for color correction. Although it seems intuitive to use Photoshop for this process, that would require editing each layer (drawing) individually, which would add a considerable amount of time to production. With After Effects, we can adjust all facets of the color and contrast over large sequences of footage.

Chapter 10

POSTPRODUCTION

wild animal act

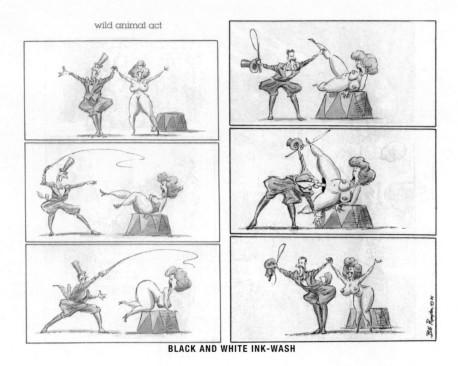

BLACK AND WHITE INK-WASH

Editing

As you're probably aware, I began my art career as a print cartoonist, and my love was sequential cartoons. In other words, I drew a lot of six- to nine-panel cartoon stories.

It was via this process that I learned the rudimentary rules of editing—what stays and what goes. What's important for the story, and what's not important? I learned about timing, pacing, building momentum, and surprise endings. All of these qualities are important in the process of editing a film.

In fact, when I create my storyboards, which resemble print cartoons, the editing of the film is pretty much predetermined. As opposed to a documentary film, in which only one out of every hundred shots will be used in the finished film, an animated film will probably use about 95 percent of the shots because it's been so thoroughly planned out.

In this chapter, I will discuss some editing tricks that I've learned over the years.

Timing

The value of timing is primordial in animation—and even now, I'm still learning how to use timing to my advantage.

I recently saw the wonderful Shane Acker film *9*, a stop-motion/computer adventure film. The editing on that film was amazingly fast with a lot of very quick cuts. At times, that technique was quite effective, and other times, I didn't know what I was watching. Often the cuts were so fast that it was a blur—but it left you with an almost impressionistic feel for the action. You might not be sure what you saw, but whatever it was, it was scary.

But that's not my style, as I do mostly humor. It's hard for me to do that kind of quick cutting. I need the jokes to be clear and easily read, so I tend to use much slower pacing—although at times I feel it's too slow.

ANGEL ENTERING BAR, FROM *IDIOTS AND ANGELS* (2008)

There are two good timing examples in *Idiots and Angels*. One is a scene early in the film, when Angel walks into his bar for the first time. He walks through the door and saunters up to the bar, which is only about four steps away, but I dragged it out to almost one minute of screen time. It must have been about 40 steps—why? I don't know, it just felt really cool.

It was intuitive, the rhythm of the music as it matched his footsteps, the beauty of Larry Campbell's pedal-steel guitar. It was the whole mystery of him approaching the bar, and the ambiance of the bar itself. So how can a one-minute sequence of a guy walking up to a bar be so entertaining? I can't really answer that question. All I know is that it's one of my favorite sequences in the film, and I get a lot of great comments on that scene.

THE DEATH GARAGE, FROM *IDIOTS AND ANGELS* (2008)

The second scene from *Idiots and Angels* that has important timing is the sequence in which Angel is driving home, and he parks his car in the garage. Things are going very badly for him at this point: everyone in the bar has made fun of him, and a mad, violent doctor is chasing him. So we see the garage, but Angel doesn't get out of his car—in fact, he leaves the engine running and closes the garage door. It soon dawns on the audience that he's going to try to commit suicide. Yet I keep a hold on the garage—it's one static shot of the garage, for about a minute. Now, again, you think, how can the audience sit still, watching a stupid garage? But it's the psychological drama that's going on inside the garage that's keeping the audience so involved in the shot.

What's going to happen? Is he going to die? Will someone save him? Will he give up? Then, after I've dragged that scenario out as long as I can, I show some toxic fumes seeping out of the garage window— the tension is building, the garage is probably full of exhaust fumes, and he's certainly done for. He's offed himself, maybe now he'll become a real angel—but the tension builds and builds. Remember, it's still just a picture of a decrepit garage.

I release the tension with Angel diving out of the side window, breaking the glass and coughing and gasping for air as he lays prostrate on the lawn. Wow, that's so cool! Over a minute of film that just shows a lonely garage! The rest of the story in that shot is developed though minimal sound effects and psychological fear and the imagination of the audience. I wish I could make a whole film like that.

I've found that the secret of great timing—especially in cartoons—is to treat the editing like you treat other aspects of a cartoon: exaggerating the tempo, and making a caricature of the timing, if you will. If it's a suspenseful sequence, you can really slow it down and drag it out. Make the shots longer than real life; make the audience wait. However, if it's an action sequence, speed it up and use quick cuts to push it to hyper-speed. People love it when you play with their emotions, and editing is a great way to control the audience. The exaggeration of timing can be very enjoyable.

Conflict

As I stated earlier, conflict is one of the essential ingredients in a great story, and because we're making a cartoon, we're lucky in that we can exaggerate the conflict.

We can camp it up and make it over the top, and that's okay, because it's animation! People expect it.

Let's say we have a shot of two cowboys with guns drawn in a Mexican standoff. Go ahead and exaggerate the tension-filled moments. Drag them out and use a lot of intercutting between the antagonists—zoom in on their faces, show sweat pouring down their temples, have a close-up of their grinding teeth. Show their hair standing on end, cut to a fist tightening up—it's animation, so it's okay! If this sort of thing were done in a live-action film, it would be preposterous—or a Sergio Leone film. But somehow, because it's a cartoon, it works. The more cuts and cutaways, the more intense the emotion in the film.

ARTWORK FROM MUSIC VIDEO "MEXICAN STANDOFF" (2008)

Effects

Another cool thing about computer editing is the varied number of effects available to add style and variety to the film. Before the computer, all of the camera moves and special effects had to be incorporated during the film shoot. But now, with the wide range of visual possibilities available on the computer, a whole variety store of postproduction effects has been opened up.

Let's go back to the previous shot, in which the two antagonists are staring each other down, ready to have a cowboy smackdown. How about really exaggerating the tension even more with special effects, besides the cutaways, zooms, and alternative POVs? How about dialing up the color extremes—use that bright lime green, or that crazy fluorescent ultraviolet that I warned you about? Or put in some cool shadows. Maybe go black and white and play with the positive and negative—anything to make it out of the ordinary.

Bring up the music; build it up big-time. Recycle it and tilt the images at awkward angles.

I made a film called "Santa: The Fascist Years" in 2008. I came up with the idea in the early 1970s as a Christmas card, but my folks hated the idea, so I stuffed it back into my idea folder and forgot about it. In 2008, I discovered the sketches and realized that now that I'm doing animation, it would make a perfect short.

STILL FROM "SANTA: THE FASCIST YEARS" (2008)

So, over a Thanksgiving weekend, I drew the entire four-minute film. People ask how I was able to make a film in that short of a time period. Well, I cheat—plain and simple. If you examine the film, you'll notice that there's not a lot of animation. Instead of laborious animation, I would take two drawings, alternate them on threes, then add a lot of camera effects—shakes, zooms, pans, dust, and scratched-film effects—and for some reason, the audience doesn't notice the lack of animation because the images are always moving, and it seems like a fully animated short. The film took longer than four days, by the way, to finish. We had to scan, clean, color, and add a voice track (by Matthew Modine) and music, but I think the entire process took about 20 days in total, and it went on to be one of my most successful films.

Humor

Editing for comedy is a very delicate talent. I'm not quite sure I've really got a grip on it. I'm always studying how others edit for humor—watching and learning. But my favorite example is "Guard Dog." The film is full of little episodes of the dog imagining all these terrible attacks on his master by innocuous woodland creatures.

My favorite, and also the audience's favorite, is the bull-in-the-pit gag. Now, I've seen it hundreds of times, and I think I know why it's such a success—it's the slow, mysterious buildup. In case you haven't seen it, I'll lay it out for you.

RAGING BULL SEQUENCE FROM "GUARD DOG" (2004)

The guard dog imagines that this harmless mole digs a humongous pit, then pulls a giant angry bull down into the pit. The fact that this tiny subterranean creature can control a three-ton bull is part of the humor. You acknowledge that it's building to something, so you accept the crazy premise. That's funny in itself. And then the extremely energetic mole covers the pit opening with a blanket of grass, and our dog owner comes along and falls into the pit. As he plummets down, he falls into a Ronald McDonald suit that naturally offends the bull.

As the shot fades out, the evil mole is laughing its head off to the sound of the bull eviscerating our dog walker guy.

When I storyboarded this sequence, I realized that the setup for the gag was almost as funny as the gag itself, so I timed the mole putting together this fiendish trap quite leisurely, with a lot of little details. This approach builds up the curiosity factor and also the tension. When the trap gets sprung, the punchline hits hard and fast.

It's that slow, mysterious buildup and quick release that make the joke so funny. It's actually similar to the Road Runner cartoons in terms of timing and editing.

But I look in two directions for my guidance in timing. First, the old classic comedy films, such as Warner Bros. cartoons, the Marx brothers, and Jacques Tati. After studying a lot of great comics' timing, I've built up a powerful intuition on how to cut a sequence.

The second source of knowledge is revealed when I show the rough cut to test audiences. Sometimes I'll ask people which gag doesn't work, and sometimes I'll get a sense from the quality of the laughter and response what needs to be recut in a film.

I had a number of other gags for "Guard Dog," and one of them was a particular favorite: a slug with welding goggles sharpening a blade of grass with an electric sander. Then there'd be a cut to him laying a spiral of slime on the newly sharpened grass blades. Our dog owner would get his feet stuck in the sticky slime and fall over on the ground, puncturing his body with the bloody blades of grass.

Now, I thought this was a classic gag—probably the best gag of the film. But no one laughed at it. I even tried to cut it differently, but still no laughs, so out it went. If people don't like it, out it goes, because I need my films to be a success. I need each gag to be a winner, no matter how much I like a certain joke—if it doesn't connect, out it goes! But later I can put it in the DVD extras—then maybe they'll laugh!

blows catapillar away

dog spots slug

Slug sharpens grass

Slug leaves spiral of slime

guy slips on slime

guy falls on sharpened grass

slug frightened

happy dog

ROUGH STORYBOARD OF REJECTED SLUG SEQUENCE FROM "GUARD DOG" (2004)

Reviewing the Film

Another method I use to perfect my editing is watching the film many times—not only with an audience, but also without one. After seeing a sequence played ten times in a row, little imperfections begin to appear, and I know precisely how to recut it.

Sometimes, I have to watch it 30 or 40 times to see where to edit it—I know that sounds incredibly boring, but believe me, when I take my films on tour and I'm stuck watching the same bad cut over and over, each time I want to cut off my fingers with a hot splicer.

Sometimes even a one- or two-frame adjustment can solve all the timing problems in a film. It's really amazing to me how great editing can make a mediocre film into a great film.

Sound

In the early days of my film career, I had very little money to invest in my films. So I hired myself as a sound designer. I rented a Nagra from my good friend, Phil Lee of Full House Sound Studios, and I developed a crude repertoire of my favorite sound effects: footsteps, hitting sounds, sexy kissing, and of course, the ever-popular balloon rubbing sounds. If you listen to my short "Nose Hair," you'll hear my sounds (that's even me playing the guitar on the soundtrack).

But, eventually, because of lack of time and talent, I had to delegate my sound duties to more professional personnel. And boy, am I glad I did. Some of those early films I made sound awful. When you hear the wind blowing, that's usually me blowing into the microphone—actually, that's kind of funny in a campy way.

"NOSE HAIR" (1994)

Bill, where do you find a good sound designer?

Good sound designers are very rare, and if you can find a good one, someone who can work with an indie budget, you're very lucky. Hold on to that person for dear life.

There are a number of ways to find these talented people. One is to check out the credits of other films in the short film programs and make notes of the designers who create great sounds. You can ask the director what that person is like to work with and how to contact them. Most directors are very open to helping their crew get other work—and if the sound editor (though they prefer "sound designer") is too busy, he or she can often recommend someone else.

Film schools are often great places to recruit sound designers, especially if you have a limited budget. Also, if you know what you want and how the sound should be, it's good to get someone who's open to direction and other ideas. Often the older designers tend to be a little more set in their ways and less open to suggestions.

I have one horror story to relate—I won't use his name, because I think he's still in the business. Anyway, I'd run into this guy occasionally because we had mutual friends, and he kept telling me I was a god, and how much he wanted to work with me—he'd even work for free, just to be able to work on one of my films.

A couple of years ago, my usual sound designer was busy working on a feature, so I called this guy up. I needed a soundtrack really quick to meet a festival deadline, and he said, "Great! Let's go!"

When I asked, "So, how much do you charge?" he replied, "Don't worry, it'll be great!" So I stupidly gave him my project, and after a few days, he played me the soundtrack—and it was terrible. Then he gave me a bill for $1,000, and I said, "What happened to you working for me for free?"

He replied, "Are you crazy? Why would I work for you for free? Nobody works for free!"

The festival deadline was coming up, and he wouldn't release the soundtrack, bad as it was, without payment in full. I had to pay a ransom to get my film back, but he had me in a desperate situation. I paid the damn money, and then I rehired my usual sound guy later to totally redo the soundtrack.

It was a bitter lesson, but an important one: always get an estimate on the project before you start. I usually like to pay half at the beginning and the rest after completion of the sound mix. It's very important to get a good sound mix to balance all of the different elements: voices, effects, and music.

The soundtrack for an animated film, short or feature, is very important—I believe it's even more crucial than for a live-action film. A great sound designer can control the mood and character of an animated film because there is no recorded sound from the set. All of the sounds come from other sources.

Sometimes my drawings are very minimal, even abstract, but a great designer will bring a sense of reality to the film simply by placing some key sound effects. One example is the garage suicide sequence in *Idiots and Angels,* as previously noted.

I've come to the point where I can rely more and more on the sound to tell the story and set the mood, which gives me more freedom to get more creative and stylized with the artwork. Look at my film "Nose Hair," which has very minimal visuals paired with very realistic sound—that great union makes it work.

It's the magic union of sound and art that makes the film fly.

Real versus Cartoony Sound

A big problem I see (or hear, actually) in a lot of student films is an amateurish soundtrack. Often young students think that to make something funny, they just have to put in a kazoo, or tin whistle, or lots of wacky, crazy sounds. Maybe 70 years ago, when Mickey Mouse first appeared with sound, that sort of thing was hilarious, but not now.

Or a student might appropriate the Hanna-Barbera sound effects library, thinking that's really cool. No! Perhaps it's campy, if you want camp, but it only reminds me of unfunny cartoons.

For me to laugh, I need to hear realistic sounds—I have to believe that these are real creatures in a real world. Like I said in an earlier chapter, humor comes when something shocking and unexpected happens to a normal, clichéd situation.

Just like the artwork, the sound should be very conventional—nothing too surprising. In fact, I usually tell my sound designer that he should pretend he's watching a live-action film and add the appropriate sounds.

Dolby

As a proud member of the Academy of Motion Pictures, I get to see the other animated shorts that are eligible for Oscar nominations, and I'm always amazed at the sound specs for those films. They're all Dolby or 5.1 sound (5.1 is the number of channels used for sounds).

Of the 40 or so films screened, mine is usually the only one in non-Dolby stereo. That means that the filmmakers of all of the other eligible shorts have each spent $5,000 or more on their sound system, and $5,000 is the cost of my entire film! Damn, I wish I could spend that kind of money on my sound. However, as I told you earlier, my budgets have to remain low if I'm going to make a profit on my movies.

Besides, I wonder if the general audience can tell the difference between stereo and Dolby stereo. Perhaps they can, but does that diminish the enjoyment or popularity of a film? I'm betting $5,000 that it doesn't—but you be the judge.

Music

It's impossible to overestimate the value of great music to an animated film. There's something so beautiful, and almost religious, about the union of great visuals and the exact, right piece of music.

Some of the classic examples: *Fantasia*, of course, "The Rabbit of Seville" and "What's Opera, Doc?" (Bugs Bunny), *Yellow Submarine* (Beatles), "Feet of Song" by Erica Russell, "The Band Concert" (Mickey Mouse), "Minnie the Moocher" (Cab Calloway and the Fleischer brothers), "Coal Black and de Sebben Dwarves" (Bob Clampett), and *American Pop* (Ralph Bakshi).

My earliest example is the film "Your Face." I knew I wanted the guy to sing a song—but what kind of song? I'd worked with Maureen McElheron for years—in the 1970s, I played pedal steel guitar (badly) in her band around clubs and bars in NYC. So when I needed music for the guy to sing, I asked her to pen a song.

Her first composition was haunting and gorgeous, and it probably would have been a hit, except it was too beautiful. The character in "Your Face" was a dork, a square—so I needed him to sing a real cornball-type love song. So we worked together on changing the lyrics, but kept the haunting melody. One line that I really liked—"Your face makes me a happy fella, no more singing a cappella"—was the exact kind of cornball lyrics that I thought the film needed.

At the time, I had no money to hire a male singer, so I hired Maureen to sing the song and play the piano, and we slowed down the track to something like a third of the original speed. And this gave the song a very eerie, nostalgic quality, like it was a song from the 1930s sung by Rudy Vallee.

Believe it or not, the song became a hit. They played it on some New Jersey radio stations, and some people even used it for their wedding promenade song!

AT THE OSCARS IN 1988 WITH MAUREEN MCELHERON

IDIOTS AND ANGELS (2008)

My film *Idiots and Angels,* being my first feature film without dialogue, required the utmost in musical support. In essence, the music *became* the dialogue—it would communicate the thoughts and feelings of the characters.

However, looking back on the film, I believe I may have used a bit too much music; in my insecurity, I was compensating for the lack of dialogue.

My process for selecting music is a bit complicated. First, while creating the drawings, I'll listen to random CDs to get me in the mood. As I travel around the world, people often hand me music that they've recorded, in the hopes that I will use it in my

films. I like that because I'm always open to hearing new songs and new styles.

Also, if I go to a concert or a club, I often buy the band's CDs to listen to at home while I draw. I've even bought music from NYC street musicians and subway performers, and some of it is quite good and exciting.

As I'm drawing the film, I'll imagine the music with the completed animated sequence—how would it fit in? Would it enhance or detract from the shot?

Ironic Music

When selecting music, don't just use your music to echo what you're seeing on the screen. Sometimes it's more interesting to be ironic. Look for music that's in contrast to the action you're seeing— maybe some light, romantic music for a battle scene, or something very heavy and dramatic for a love scene.

In *Idiots and Angels,* during the violent battle scene with Angel, I played some church choir music that added a nice counterpoint. It brought a lot of spirituality to the sequence. In *Hair High,* there's a very brutal football sequence in which players are being massacred on the field of play—I put in a light, airy, romantic French song.

HAIR HIGH (2004)

Such an unexpected choice of music can put more emphasis on the shot, and in fact can make it more dramatic and more memorable. But use this ironic technique sparingly—it can easily be overdone, too, so be careful.

One firm rule of mine is to not use any kind of electronic or synthetic music, which I hate. I prefer music using real, uncomputerized sounds.

Music Budgeting

When I'm choosing music for my films, I try to stay away from the big-name acts—there's no way I can afford a famous band. Therefore, I have a lot of musician friends whose music I use, and they also suggest other talented musicians.

ME, MAUREEN MCELHERON, AND HANK BONES AT A *HAIR HIGH* MUSICAL SESSION (2003)

In fact, Hank Bones, who's created a lot of great music for my films (especially the wonderful soundtrack for *Hair High*) would often have big backyard music parties, and all these fabulous talented musicians would perform. They were like big country hootenannies, and I've met a lot of my favorite musicians at these wonderful events.

I then have a large stack of CDs with tracks that I want to use in my film. But how much do I pay?

The total music budget for *Idiots and Angels* was set at $10,000. Now, I know that sounds very low, and it is, but I was really broke at that time (in fact, I'm still broke as I write this), and I could barely afford that. I wanted to use about 30 songs, so you can see that works out to about $300 per song.

Now, I was able to get by with some freebies. The John Philip Sousa march I wanted to use was performed by the US Marine Band, and it was very old, so it was in public domain (plus, as a military recording, the US taxpayers own it). Another track was by an old cartoonist friend of mine, and he donated the song to the film. But happy accidents like these are very rare.

Most of the musicians I contacted grumbled about the $300 fee, but eventually they made the decision to accept it because they felt it would give their song some exposure, and perhaps they'd make extra money when the film eventually played on TV. Royalties like this are paid by a cable TV station to the songwriters through ASCAP or BMI and don't cost me a thing!

How to Save Money

I'm going to cite five interesting examples of how I got some of my music for *Idiots and Angels*.

Example #1: I love the band Pink Martini. They're from my hometown of Portland, and their music was perfect for my film—very evocative and emotional. The good news was that I'd known the band's leader, Thomas Lauderdale, since he got out of college—he did a very funny cameo appearance in my second live-action film, *Guns on the Clackamas,* in 1985; also, my talented brother Peter is the band's sound engineer. So I get to see the band whenever they perform in New York, and we all hang out after.

In fact, there is a nice kinship between Pink Martini and me—they travel a lot (like me), they're totally independent (like me), and they produce and distribute their CDs to huge success (unlike me, but I'm working on that). So they've been very supportive of my films, and they charge me a very fair price for their music.

Example #2: The opening and closing song for *Idiots and Angels,* which features Whistling Geert, is very important because it's a unique song that's very compatible to my film. I met Whistling Geert at the Florida Film Festival; he was there from Holland with a documentary about him being the whistling champion of the world. Well, we got drunk together, and as I listened to his music, I boldly claimed that

I wanted to use that one particular song for my next film—and he said, "Yeah, great, no problem!"

However, his producer had different ideas—he wanted $8,000 for the rights to that song! Whoa, that was almost my entire music budget! I think he assumed that since I was making a film in the United States, it must be a big Hollywood film for which those kinds of budgets are normal. After I explained that this was certainly not a Hollywood film, but in fact an indie film with a lower budget, and then begged and pleaded on my knees (it was on a long-distance phone call, but I think he knew I was on my knees), he came down to $5,000—still way too much.

So I called back the next day, and I offered all kinds of incentives to get him to meet my price. I said I'd give him a piece of art from the film, plus I'd create his next CD cover and I'd even create a music video for the band. Well, I guess that was the final deal maker, or else he just felt sorry for me, because we signed the deal for just a bit over my normal rate.

Example #3: Tom Waits. While I was drawing *Idiots and Angels,* I listened to a lot of his music to get me in the mood of the bar scenes. His songs just evoke a lot of that barfly culture—so many of them are about drinking and its consequences. This kind of approach is really dangerous, because you can get to a point where you fall in love with some music, and you absolutely have to have it, even though you probably can't afford it—well, that's what happened to me.

I don't know Tom Waits personally, I've never met him, and I've heard that he's very reclusive. But I do know Jim Jarmusch, and I know they go back to Jarmusch's film *Down By Law,* so I sent Jim a rough cut of *Idiots and Angels* and asked if he could pass it along to Mr. Waits.

Well, after about a month of not hearing anything, I figured the deal was off. Then I got a nice email from Tom's wife saying that he loved my film, and I could have any song I wanted for it. Yee-hah! There *was* a Santa Claus! Of course, I still had to pay for the song rights, but it was at a reduced rate (one that just barely fit within my budget). Still, I was ecstatic.

It just shows you what a cool guy Tom Waits is—he likes to support projects that are interesting and show an affinity to his music.

Example #4: One of my favorite scenes in *Idiots and Angels* is the one with the guy entering the bar, which I talked about earlier. It's so beautiful that I wanted to get the top pedal steel player in the United States—no, make that the world. So I called up Larry Campbell. Now, Larry and I go way back; he did a couple of steel guitar riffs for the Wiseman segment in my first animated feature, *The Tune.*

This was back in 1991—Larry was new in town and very accommodating. Well, since then he's become a steel guitar superstar, working for people like Levon Helm, Bob Dylan, and Emmylou Harris (more about her later). When I called Larry, he said he was way too busy touring, working on an album, and doing some commercials. But I sent him a rough cut of the film, with temporary music by Daniel Lanois, so he could (hopefully) fall in love with it.

I always use temp music because it really helps to get a feel for the mood and tempo of the film—also, it helps when I show people the rough cut, in that it gives them a better idea about the finished product. However, I do recall that one time I used some temp music from Cirque du Soleil on a rough cut of *Hair High,* and two weeks later I got a call from their lawyers, asking me for $5,000 for the use of that song.

I don't know how they heard that I used their song as a temporary track, but I guess those lawyers are ever-vigilant. I showed the piece to only a few people! So I told them that it was only in there to get a feel for the emotion, that I'd never include it in the final film without permission, or sell it or show it at a festival or on TV. Also, I agreed to immediately take it out of the film, and the lawyers went away.

Anyway, I kept pestering Larry Campbell, and finally he said that in about three weeks, he'd have an hour of time for me. Wow, one hour! So, when the time came, I picked him up, with his steel guitar, and we grabbed a cab down to the sound session, arranged by my sound designer, Greg Sextro. We got him set up, he recorded the song in two takes, and I gave him money for a cab home. I think he made it back with five minutes to spare. I had to pay him a little extra, because he's Larry Campbell, but you know what? It was worth it, because that scene became a knockout!

And the last musical story I'll tell you happened when I was at the Sundance Festival. I think I was screening *I Married a Strange Person* there. I was at a party one night, and when I turned around, standing behind me was Emmylou Harris—Emmy-friggin'-lou Harris!

EMMYLOU HARRIS, ME, AND MARY KAY PLACE, ACTRESS AND SINGER, AT SUNDANCE (1998)

She's my country goddess—I've listened to more of her music than anyone else's, even the Beatles. I nervously introduced myself to her, and I told her I was an animator. That didn't get much of a rise out of her, so I told her it was my greatest wish to use some of her music in one of my movies. Again, that didn't seem to cause too much enthusiasm on her part—she probably hears that a lot.

I asked for her address, to send her some of my work, and she gave me her agent's contact information. Wow! I was so excited. I figured if she liked my animation, she might let me use a song. So as soon as I returned to New York, I mailed off a package containing every film and book I ever made. And ... I never heard back from her.

I think what happened was that I came off as a complete stalker, and she probably told her agent to trash anything that came in the mail from some crazy person named Bill Plympton. But one day—you never know.

The trick is to keep your music budget as low as possible. You can often get better music, and more rights, from an undiscovered or up-and-coming musical act than from a more established band.

Some bands are so excited to see their music set to animation that they may even pay you and use the scene as a sort of music video. I recommend haunting all the local music clubs and small concert halls and making friends with a lot of musicians. This is how you can find great music at a great price.

Also, you can tell them that when the film plays on TV, they'll get some fat royalty money, as long as they're registered with ASCAP or BMI.

Film Composers

I work with a number of composers—Maureen McElheron, Hank Bones, Corey Jackson, and Nicole Renaud—and my working relationship with each of them is pretty much the same. I send them the storyboards or rough art of the pencil test so that they can get an idea of the film; then we discuss musical ideas, instrumentation, tempo, and size of ensemble.

I may have some of their music already on the sample reel or some other piece of music as a temp track. Then, after a few weeks, they'll play me a rough version of what they had in mind and we'll discuss how it works with the story and picture. Then they'll go back and do a finished piece of music.

Hopefully, the finished music will sync up with the film—if not, we have two options: change the speed of the music, or retime the animation. In any case, getting the music to time up with the picture is of paramount importance.

It's such a great feeling to witness a film in which the music and picture compliment each other.

NICOLE RENAUD, COLOR PENCIL (2010)

Music Clearances

Before you can use a piece of music in your film, you have to get the rights, also known as music clearances. Performance rights refers to the actual recorded music on a CD, and clearing this music often means negotiating with the record label or a manager or a producer.

Then there are publishing rights, which refer to the composition of the song itself, and getting these cleared means negotiating with the songwriter. Sometimes the songwriter is also the performer, but not always, and sometimes you have to talk to the writer's management instead.

Whenever possible, I try to deal directly with the performer or songwriter, because he or she is usually much more willing to make a deal than lawyers or agents are. Sometimes it seems like the lawyers are trying to prevent the use of a song, rather than encourage it.

Also, it's very important to get all film usage rights initially in all territories for perpetuity. If you only buy festival rights at a cheap price, and then your film becomes a hit, the lawyers smell money and will jack up the price for the theatrical rights because they know you're desperate to make a deal.

A lot of filmmakers use music in the public domain—this is most often older music with copyrights that have expired. Perhaps the most successful of these filmmakers is Don Hertzfeldt, famous animator of the short "Rejected." Check out Don's films if you haven't already. He's the only other guy I know who regularly makes a profit on his short films—and that's maybe because his films are very cheap to make. They're essentially stick-figure cartoons, for Christ's sake.

Don draws and shoots all the animation himself and records the voices and sound effects. Hell, he probably makes his own prints in his darkroom lab. But he's very effective in using classical music that has passed into the public domain. This is a great way to get some of the best music ever recorded—Mozart, Beethoven, Brahms—for almost free. You might just have to pay a small fee for the recording rights, and it will be yours in perpetuity. You can find a lot of classical music available on the Internet, at sites like sounddogs.com.

For examples of music contracts, you can go to http://www.musiccontracts101.com/docs/sample/.

WITH DON HERTZFELDT AND MIKE JUDGE IN NYC

Testing

I read once that Steven Spielberg hates to test his films—that he has to be forced to prescreen his films before releasing them. Now, I'm a huge fan of

Spielberg, but I swear by testing my films. It's certainly not an enjoyable exercise, but it's extremely useful. If I've spent three years and $200,000 on a film, I want to make damn sure that it will be popular with the audience. And the only way to do that is to get feedback—lots of feedback.

There's nothing worse than going to a screening of your finished film and watching it completely flop in front of an audience—by that time, it's too expensive to make any beneficial changes. So you'd better be certain that what you're sending out to the festivals and theaters is as good as it can be.

For me, it starts with the storyboard. I have a few very close friends in the business who understand storyboards. I show them the completed storyboard, in hopes of getting some suggestions on how to make it better. I figure that if changes need to be made, that's definitely the cheapest time to make them.

The next stage for testing is after the pencil test is done. I'll often put temp music, voices, and basic effects on the film and show it around. My pencil

tests are pretty tight; I include a lot of shading and detail, so it won't take a lot of imagination to see what might be wrong with the film. Sometimes I'll even get a large audience to view this version.

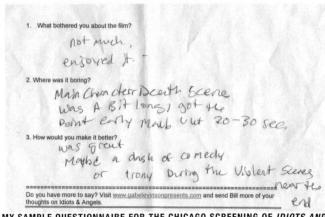

MY SAMPLE QUESTIONNAIRE FOR THE CHICAGO SCREENING OF *IDIOTS AND ANGELS* (2007)

In 2007, I was able to show a pencil-test version of *Idiots and Angels* to a large crowd at the great Music Box Theatre in Chicago. We had an audience of about 300 people, and they filled out questionnaires about the plot, the characters, and what worked and what didn't, which was very helpful. Of course, there were some whackos who missed the mark completely or didn't get what I was trying to say—those surveys I tossed out. But when there was a consensus about a problem, I paid very close attention and tried to resolve it.

Finally, when the film is finished, colored, sound-mixed, and ready to go to the lab, I'll show a DVD to another audience, and of course I'll watch it numerous times myself. There's still time at that stage to make it better, and I definitely want to send out the best product I can.

It's also instructive to show the film to a small group of strangers and then talk to them after the screening and ask them more direct questions, probing their deeper feelings about the film. At this type of showing I get really good, impartial criticism and perhaps learn the reasons why they don't like certain parts of my movie.

To me, testing is essential to the success of a film, no matter what Mr. Spielberg says.

Chapter 11

SELLING YOUR FILM

In 1987, I took my first animated film, "Your Face," to the Annecy Festival in France. I'd been there two years before with "Boomtown," a film I directed but did not produce—but "Your Face" was a very different beast; it was funny and quirky, while "Boomtown" was serious and political.

I had no idea how "Your Face" would play to European audiences, because it was such a goofball film. Well, the European audiences loved the film. What a great relief for me—afterward, people came up to congratulate me, which was another wild shock. But the most astounding experience came when buyers approached me, offering money for the film. I had thought that the film would end up being an amusing little trifle, but with Spanish TV offering $4,000, France's Canal Plus willing to pay $5,000, and the BBC putting up $3,000—what the hell? This film was going to make money! Suddenly I liked the festival circuit.

Many filmmakers think that once they've finished their film, they just have to send it off to MTV or the Cartoon Network, and they'll be discovered. Not so fast! It just doesn't work that way—I used to visit Abby Terkuhle's office, back when he was in charge of MTV Animation, and he had videos of unsolicited short films stacked up to the ceiling. He told me that's how many he would get in just one week!

Now, there was no way he could watch all of those unsolicited tapes—besides, most of them were probably crap anyway. So where did he go to see all of the great animated shorts? He went to the festivals, because their selection process would filter out all of the crappy films. In five days in an exotic locale, he could watch the crème de la crème and write the whole thing off as a business expense.

So unless you have an uncle that works for HBO or you're sleeping with the president of the Sundance Channel, my advice to you is to go the festival route.

Here's my list of the top ten festivals:

1. The Oscars. I know, it's not a festival, but it is open to every filmmaker. You just have to play your film in Los Angeles County for a week or win the top prize at an Academy-approved festival, then fill out a form and your film can qualify.

Whenever the press writes about me, they usually include the phrase "Oscar-nominated," because that's the industry seal of approval. So it's probably the most important event in a filmmaker's life. And anyone can apply; it's very democratic.

If you do get nominated (or even if your film makes the "short list"), you can get any meeting you want in Hollywood. You can get an agent, tons of press and distribution—you've got it made!

Plus, the Oscars are by far the best party you'll ever go to.

2. Cannes. The Cannes Festival is like the Oscars in many ways, but it also has topless women on the beaches. The French are animation-crazy, so—as with the Oscars—you'll get beaucoup press and sales, and you'll get to walk the great red carpet! But please try to learn French.

3. Sundance. They now have an animation program that is very popular. For a week every January, Park City is swarming with agents looking to put a purpose to their ski trip. And there's tons of press and distributors there, so it's high on my to-enter list.

4. Annecy. This is my favorite festival. I go every year, regardless of whether I have a new film (I usually do). It's held in this quaint medieval village at the foot of the beautiful French Alps. There are lovely canals flowing into the Lac d'Annecy, with picturesque swans everywhere. They have great restaurants in which you could be sitting next to Nick Park or Jan Svankmeyer or John Lasseter, or—if you're really lucky—maybe even Bill Plympton. And everyone is very approachable and friendly.

ANNECY VILLAGE

The French fans are very passionate about films—if they don't like your film, they'll boo and throw balls of paper at you. But if your film is popular, they treat you like a god! Plus, the place is filled with buyers from all over the world looking for short, funny films. The Market, or MIFA, is at a nearby exclusive hotel; this is where all the deals are done.

5. The Annie Awards. The Annies, which are organized by ASIFA Hollywood, are to me the Oscars

of animation. Because they take place in Los Angeles, the mecca of the animation world, it's a super place to hang out with all of the greats in the industry. I never miss a chance to go to the Annie Awards—and winning one is extremely prestigious.

6. Clermont-Ferrand. This is another great French film festival, but it's for shorts only. They tend to prefer live action, but they also show animation. Unlike Annecy, it's held in a boring industrial town (they make Michelin tires there), but the people are mad for short films. They have five very large cinemas, seating up to 2,000 people each—and they are packed to the gills for every show, all day long! When do these people work? Consequently, this festival has become a huge market for short films.

Even if my film is not selected for competition, they will put it in their Bibliotheque (library) and it will make sales, even though it wasn't screened—amazing. Be warned, though, this festival prefers more avant-garde films, so humor rarely makes it to the big screen.

7. Ottawa Animation Festival. The Canadians have a very active animation culture supported by the Canadian Film Board. They also have a very popular festival each year in Ottawa, run by Chris Robinson, whose specialty is Estonian films, and scratch-on-film movies—so you can get an idea of the kind of films they like, which are dark and experimental. But they also have a market, which has become very important for directors and producers. It's also an especially wonderful festival for students.

8. Stuttgart Animation Festival. Another one of my favorites. It's held in a beautiful part of the Old City next to a lovely park with lots of fountains and beer gardens. The festival is very well run, with great programs of popular Hollywood animation, plus historic programs of obscure films, European features, great parties, and also packed audiences.

9. Expression en Corto. This Mexican festival takes place in two cities, San Miguel De Allende and Guanajuato. It's probably the largest market festival for shorts in the burgeoning Latin American market. They have a wide variety of programs, both

live action and animation. They have press and buyers from all over the world—it's truly an international festival, and I highly recommend it.

10. Sitges. Situated on a beautiful seaside town just south of Barcelona, Spain, it's become a great market for fantasy and animated films. The food is fantastic! The location is exotic—you can swim in the ocean every morning, and the Spanish audiences are also rabid fans! Also, the festival is full of press and buyers—you'll have a ball!

Market Festivals

This list is for festivals that are important for business—they also have great parties and social activities, but I go primarily for business:

1. Tribeca Film Festival. Started by Robert De Niro and Jane Rosenthal after 9/11, this festival in downtown New York has become a great event in just a few short years. It's great for finding distribution, but it's too bad that they tend to treat the filmmakers like crap.

2. Toronto Worldwide Shorts Festival. Not to be confused with the much larger Toronto Film Festival (which doesn't allow shorts from outside Canada), the Shorts Festival has become a very important marketplace for short films and animation.

3. Palm Springs Shorts Festival. Not to be confused with the Palm Springs International Film Festival, this festival is very well run. They have a lot of buyers and press, plus great parties—I've done a lot of deals through this festival, and met a lot of really great people.

4. Deauville American Film Festival. It seems like France is full of great film festivals. Another favorite is the Deauville American Film Festival—it's located in the Normandy region. Lots of old money, beautiful beaches, and Belle Époque charm. One time after swimming in the ocean I walked through the private garden to my room in the stately hotel, and there were Tom Hanks and Steven Spielberg, just hanging out and drinking aperitifs. I would have introduced myself, but I looked like a drowned rat emerging from the seaside.

5. AFI. The American Film Institute festival is quite important in terms of programming. Running parallel to this festival is the prestigious American Film Market, so it's possible to sell your film in both events. The festival takes place in Los Angeles, so it's a great place to hold industry meetings.

6. Fantasia Festival. Another Canadian Festival, this one in Montreal, which attracts huge audiences. It's particularly interested in fantasy and Asian films (hence the name), but they love animation—check it out.

7. Aspen Shorts Festival. This very well-organized festival, like Palm Springs, is one of the biggest US festivals devoted to short films. Both are very good places to pick up distribution; it's also held in a very lovely but expensive town.

8. Göteburg Festival. This Swedish festival is like the Clermont-Ferrand of Scandinavia; it's an old and established festival that gets tons of press and distributors.

9. Hong Kong Film Festival. If you want to get into the huge Asian market, this is the one for you. It's a very old and well-respected festival, and press, buyers, and other festival directors come from all over—China, Korea, Japan—to see the new films, so you should check it out.

10. Puchon International Student Animation Festival (PISAF) and Seoul International Cartoon and Animation Festival. These are two Korean festivals that spotlight animation. I love Korea; they are my biggest Asian market, and they love fantasy and animation.

11. Animator Festival in Poznan. This is a real up-and-coming festival in Poland. There's a lot of great animation coming out of Poland, and this is the place to see it.

12. Animafest Zagreb. This once-mighty festival in Croatia used to be very important, but because of war and money issues, it's lost a lot of its luster. It's coming back strong, though. Zagreb is a beautiful old city that holds many wonderful charms.

Fun Festivals

Festivals can be more than just places to sell your film. Following is a list of fun festivals, with great parties and beautiful scenery:

1. Woodstock Film Festival. I've been affiliated with this festival for about ten years, and I keep coming back because they treat the filmmakers so well. Also, it's held in a beautiful preserved village with lots of great parties and people.

2. Florida Film Festival. Like Woodstock, they know how to treat filmmakers. Great programming and wonderful parties, with terrific ambience in the cinema and restaurant at the Enzian Theater. Check out the huge jungle mural in the Eden Bar, created by moi.

3. Monstra in Lisbon, Portugal. I had a ball there; it's such a beautiful city. The cinema is this historic old movie palace that's been refurbished, and the people are so nice and obsessed with animation. And it's near the ocean, in case you want to take a swim.

4. Anima Mundi. This one takes place in beautiful Rio de Janeiro (you'll notice a lot of my favorite festivals take place in warm climates near beaches). This festival is getting larger every year. It's well run, with a very enthusiastic following of young film students.

5. San Sebastian Horror Festival. Not to be confused with the regular San Sebastian Film Festival. Held in another beautiful Spanish town in Basque country, on the Atlantic coast, with fabulous food and great parties. They love weird animated films, so I felt right at home here.

6. Martha's Vineyard Film Festival. A gem of a festival, in a beautiful seaside village. You might run into President Obama there.

7. KROK. A crazy Russian festival that takes place on a boat. The films never start on time, the projection is always haphazard, and the food is not the best, but you can drink vodka, party, and sing every night as the giant ship cruises past the lovely Ukrainian countryside. Believe me, it's an experience you'll never forget.

8. Telluride Film Festival. One of the most prestigious festivals in the world. On top of the
beautiful Rocky Mountains, it literally takes your
breath away (you're over a mile high). The best
programming in the world, and all of the stars
are there. I've had a tough time getting my films
accepted—twice in 25 years—but if you get in,
it's worth it. The best parties ever, and the press
is frowned upon—it's not a market festival.

9. Ashland Film Festival. Situated in the gorgeous
Southern Oregon Valley, this historic town is a
wonderful place for a film festival. Great programming and terrific parties—you'll love it!

10. ASIFA New York. I guess I have a fondness
for this festival, because it's right in my own
backyard, and everyone I know in the New York
animation society is usually there. And the party
afterward is fantastic, because you get to mingle
with all of the animators! And it's free!

If you remember my earliest experience with ASIFA
and "Your Face" from previous chapters, then you
know the special fondness I have for that organization.

I'd like to explain about ASIFA, because it was
through that organization that I got my start. ASIFA
is a French acronym that stands for Association
Internationale du Film d'Animation. It was started
in the 1960s and has grown to become truly international, with chapters on every continent (except
Antarctica). The United States alone has around ten
active chapters.

The largest is in Los Angeles, simply because
there is such a huge animation industry there.
And it's there that they hold the prestigious Annie
Awards (the Oscars of animation).

The New York chapter is geared more toward
independent animation, simply because New York
has the largest collection of indie animators in the

ME, JERRY BECK, AND DAN O'SHANNON ON THE ANNIE AWARDS RED CARPET

to make prints? Where should I go to sell my film? Which are the coolest film festivals? All of these questions, and more, can be answered through ASIFA.

Also, as a social organization, it's a great group of people to hang out with, party, and talk about what exciting new films are in production. I heartily recommend that you join an ASIFA chapter in your area. It will give you tons of inspiration to get on with your next film.

Comic Conventions

Another big market for my films is the comic conventions—these places are not great for finding distributors, but they are great places for making press and industry connections. Also, I usually make a few bucks selling DVDs and art. Here are my favorites:

world. We gather every month to watch films or listen to lectures. But for me, the most important aspect of ASIFA is as a resource for information about the animation business.

Where can I find a cheap animation table? Who are some good voice-over talents? What's the best lab

1. San Diego Comic-Con. The granddaddy of them all. They have a small film festival within the convention, and I enter every year, though I've never won—how frustrating! But San Diego is still a great place to see everyone from Hollywood.

KEVIN, ALEXIA, JOHN, LUCY SPAIN, AND ME AT THE SAN DIEGO COMIC-CON

2. New York Comic-Con. This is a relatively new event, but it's growing fast. People say that in a few years, it may compare to San Diego. The price of a booth is a lot more affordable than in San Diego—and for me, it's certainly more convenient.

3. MoCCA. The Museum of Comic and Cartoon Art hosts an Art Festival each year, and this event is more for the underground and independent comics and graphic novels. So it actually has a lot of my fans there—I love this event, and I'll occasionally do a panel there.

There are dozens of great comic conventions around America—also check out the one in Angouleme, France. Many of them support animation, so be sure to go online and find out which ones have animation sections.

How to Find the Right Festival

The Internet is a great place to discover thousands of festivals—there's even a film festival in Sweden that focuses on pain—so if you have a film that's all about pain, send it to Sweden. Check out the website Without A Box for more information on festivals.

But be careful: a lot of them charge submission fees. The European festivals, because they're state-sponsored, are usually free to enter; most of the US festivals charge a nominal fee of $15 to $40. Some charge more, up to $100—those I would strongly encourage to avoid because they're ripoffs.

The good news is that if you've won a prize before at these festivals, or if they show a lot of your films, sometimes, if you ask real nicely, you might be able to get a waiver of the entry fee.

And if you have a feature film that's popular and getting a lot of publicity, sometimes it's even possible to get a screening fee from the festivals—I've done it a few times. I sometimes feel awkward asking for a screening fee, because I should be happy to have my film in any festival, but you have to remember that they charge the public admission to see the film, so it seems only fair.

Okay, let's say you get accepted to a big important festival like Sundance. This is a festival where a lot of films are picked up for distribution, and there will be tons of press. How do you prepare for this intense week of marketing?

First, I think if you have a feature playing at the festival, it's good to have a press agent. There are a lot of press agents around; just ask other filmmakers whom they recommend.

It's tough to know how much to pay a press agent—in my experience, anywhere from $1,000 to $10,000 is the proper range—but just remember that if you pay on the low end of the scale, they'll probably be handling other films along with yours, and those other films might get a lot more attention.

To help the press agent, I always put together some press packets, filled with:

- A postcard with an intriguing image on the front and showing on the back the cast, credits, a synopsis, screening times and places, and of course contact information. These cards are invaluable; I print up about 2,000 and give them to anyone I talk to so they can tell their friends about the screening.
- A more complete synopsis, plus some interesting anecdotes or background stories about the film's production. This additional material could be some information about famous people whose

voices are in the film or any notable musicians on the soundtrack.

- A complete list of the credits; the reviewers absolutely have to h ave this. A short clip or promotional trailer from the film on DVD is great, too, along with some stills.

ME WITH LIFE-SIZE *MUTANT ALIENS* PROMOTIONAL MONSTER COSTUME AND BRIAN HAIMES, THE SUIT'S CREATOR

Posters are important, too—you can use the same image from the postcard so that people won't get confused or think there are two films with the same name.

Finally, it would be great to have some swag, or gifts, to hand out—some that I've used to great effect are film strips—often when the lab makes a film print, the color could be off or the sound could be out of sync. I ask for these rejected prints, and then cut them up into little sections, then put those in fancy tiny envelopes. I autograph the front and give them away—you'd be surprised how popular they are.

You can also get these tiny film viewers, little plastic ones with a clear window at one end. I cut up the old or damaged film prints and put single frames of film inside (it's best if the scene has some nudity or violence—I have no idea why) and give those away. The promotional companies that make the viewers can even sometimes add the name of the film on the side—people love that stuff.

But the most effective giveaway is for me to make a drawing of one of my star characters on the back of the postcards I hand out—people go batshit crazy for that!

The Tune Deal

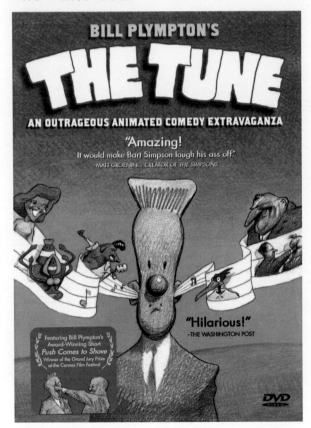

Along with the press agent, the most important person to have on your side at these events is a sales agent.

When I took my first feature film *The Tune* to Sundance, I was very lucky to have the great John Pierson representing my film for distribution. At that time, he was famous for repping Spike Lee, Richard Linklater, and then later Kevin Smith.

It was amazing for me to find out how the business worked—*The Tune* got huge ovations and lots of great reviews and had tons of fans, but we never got the kind of offers that we were hoping for. In fact, we had only one distributor interested in handling the film, the newbie October Films—and they were so new that they had no money to offer as an advance. I think no one at that time believed there was an audience for indie animation.

What was I to do? Put the film on the shelf and forget about it? Distribute it myself? Or take their offer and risk not making a dime?

Well, obviously we took October Films' offer, such as it was. The film did all right, but I made absolutely no money from October or from TV sales or from the video release. It was only after October's contract ran out, and the rights reverted back to me, that I was able to make some money in the United States on that film.

ME AND JOHN PIERSON, MEETING BEFORE THE L.A. PREMIERE OF *THE TUNE*

The *Strange Person* Deal

The other distribution deal I got was from Lionsgate Films for my second animated feature, *I Married a Strange Person*. This deal was negotiated by Catherine Branscome, my sales agent, and it was a much sweeter deal than October's. We got just under a six-figure advance; plus, the film did so well that I actually got royalties. Imagine that: royalties!

So, it does pay to have a sales rep or agent with you at the festivals. Their usual cut is between 10 percent to 30 percent of the deal, depending on what your relationship is.

This is a very difficult question; I still don't have a definitive answer, but let me give you my thoughts.

The prevailing philosophy is absolutely no! Don't let any press or distributors see the film before the world premiere; otherwise, you'll lose your excitement factor.

You want all the buyers there at your premiere screening in order to build up a buzz and bring the distribution to a frenzied buying spree. However, what happens if you get a very sullen audience that day or there's a blizzard outside and only a few people show up? (This is what happened to me with *Mutant Aliens*). Then the film bombs! Big mistake.

You sometimes hear about a lot of films getting picked up before the festival. How do the buyers get their screeners? What's going on? Often, a filmmaker or a sales agent will have a cozy relationship with a distributor, and they may show them the film at the editing stage in order to get the distributor excited and to secure an advance of some funds to finish the film. This happens all the time, so letting people see the film before the screening can be useful, and there really is no right or wrong way. Both methods are a gamble, but isn't the film business always a gamble?

I've heard stories—I don't know if they're true—that aggressive distributors curry favors with the heads of the festivals in order to get an insider's look at the hot films before the selection is announced.

Telluride Story

Back in 1987, I was invited to go to the Telluride Film Festival with my animated short "How to Kiss." It was a huge thrill for me, seeing all these great films and meeting all these great filmmakers, such as Chuck Jones. But the most amazing event happened after the premiere of Louis Malle's film *Au Revoir Les Enfants*.

We all went out to the Sheridan Opera House restaurant after the screening, and at each small table was a group of acquisition heads from independent film companies like Miramax and New Line Cinema—there were about seven tables full of buyers. Mr. Malle entered with his agent, grabbed an empty table, and each one of the distributors patiently awaited their turn to be invited to sit at his table and make their offer to the hot director.

MAIN STREET, TELLURIDE, COLORADO (PHOTO BY SANDRINE FLAMENT)

As I sat at the bar, I thought, "Damn, that's what I want! I want to make a film that has the buyers lining up to meet with me." Well, I still haven't done that—but there's still time. I'm still waiting at my table. Unfortunately, it's an empty restaurant and no one's rushing to join me for dinner.

The Distribution Deal

Let's assume that you've made a great film, and you've got a distributor hot to handle your film—what's next? Hopefully, your sales rep can take over for you, and make the deal ... not so fast there, young Orson Welles! You've got to define what you want.

Before I talk about contracts, I need to make a little disclaimer—I'm not a lawyer, I don't like contracts, and it's probably better for you to get a lawyer (or a more thorough book on the subject) that specializes in the details of entertainment law—but I can give you a few of the important points that I look for:

1. GTFM. Get The Friggin' Money. Try to get money up front. It's much harder to get companies to pay you after the film has opened.

2. Try to get a gross participation, not net. In other words, you should get some money (royalties) before the distributor starts deducting all of their expenses—prints, advertising, travel, hotel, printing, and so on (good luck on this one).

3. Be sure there's a performance clause in there stating that if they don't release the film, after a prescribed time (one year, for example) all rights revert back to you—you don't want the film gathering dust on a lonely shelf somewhere.

4. Try to get a commitment on a release budget so that you know that the feature will get its proper release. Say, anywhere from $30,000 to $1 million.

5. Try to limit the territory so that you can get rights to sell to the lucrative overseas markets.

How do you find the right distributor?

Proceed very carefully—there are dozens of distribution companies out there. When you start working the festival circuit, you'll become familiar with them. They're at all of the parties, on panels, at the screenings. Be friendly and make connections; they're very important people. Buy them drinks and give them DVDs.

Also, read the trades, like *Variety*, *Hollywood Reporter*, *Cartoon Brew*, and *AWN*—they have all of the news about indie distributors. Keep a list of the films you like and who distributed them. Find out who the acquisition people are for those companies, then take their cards and put their contact information in your address book.

Distributor Complaints

I've got a couple of gripes about dealing with distributors.

It's a common principle that you never reveal the budget of your film. I don't know how many panels I've gone to with indie directors blabbing on about how great their film is—then, during the Q&A, someone always asks about the budget, which of course is what everyone wants to know. The director either says that he doesn't know, which of course is bullshit, or that he can't say—why the hell not?

The usual answer is that the distributors supposedly base their advance offers on how big the budget is. Now, I know a lot of acquisition people, and I've never heard anyone say that the budget determines the advance. It's the quality and sales potential of the film that determines the advance—if there is an advance.

Example #1: *The Blair Witch Project*, supposedly made for just $10,000, got a huge advance. The distributor thought it could do well theatrically, because of all the great buzz and publicity.

By contrast, there are countless other "indie films" with budgets of $10 million to $20 million that don't get anything close to that for an advance. So I see no reason why filmmakers can't be honest and tell everyone what a film cost to make. Some films, like those from Robert Rodriguez (*El Mariachi*), are so cheap that they promote the films by mentioning how low the budget was.

I'm always proud to talk about my budgets. It's very instructive to see what kind of money goes into making each different film. And I'll be honest with you: only three of my features have made their costs back, as of this writing: *The Tune, I Married a Strange Person*, and *Idiots and Angels*. See, that wasn't too difficult to say.

My other peeve is distributors' reluctance to acquire my films. It's a real mystery to me, because when the distributors see my films, they always have the same lame excuse: "It's not for us." What does that mean? I'm left to hypothesize about what "It's not for us" means.

ME AND MAUREEN MCELHERON (*THE TUNE*) AND QUENTIN TARANTINO (*RESERVOIR DOGS*) AT SUNDANCE (1992)

Is it because the film is animated? In 2010, five of the top ten grossing films were animated, and another three were very special effects–heavy films. So I know that people love animation.

Is it because the film has adult ideas, for an adult audience? The great Quentin Tarantino essentially makes live-action cartoons for adults, and they do very well at the box office.

Is it because I've taken this pristine art form, created by Walt Disney for children, and somehow sullied its good name? Is animation only an art form for kids—am I the "dirty old man" of cartoons?

Is it because my stories are not good? But people come out of the theater, after watching *Idiots and Angels,* raving about the story and the characters—and all of the reviews remarked about how interesting the story was.

Is it because my films are hand-drawn, not CGI? All of the great Disney classics were drawn by hand, and 90 percent of all the animation on TV is hand-drawn.

Or is it because I'm an independent? I don't work out of a big Hollywood studio with banks of producers, agents, and bureaucrats. Does that scare them? Do they need me to hire hundreds of artists and writers before they're comfortable selling the film to an audience? Isn't the quality of the picture the bottom line for the commercial value of a film?

It's my strong belief that the audience wants to see something different—something fresh. They want new ideas and new visions. They're hungering for a new voice in the film business, and I think I'm one of the many new storytellers. Why can't the distributors see that?

Chapter 12

SELF-DISTRIBUTION

Let's say no one wants to pick up your film for distribution. That's fair; that happens all the time. To me, most of the time.

What are your options? Put it on the shelf, toss it in the river, or self-distribution. I chose self-distribution—my films *J. Lyle, Guns on the Clackamas, Walt Curtis: The Peckerneck Poet, Mutant Aliens, Hair High, and Idiots and Angels* all ended up being self-distributed.

It's not an easy road—there are a lot of barriers and difficulties inherent in self-distribution. But I believe in my films; I know people want to see them. They're like my children, and they deserve to have a life. They should be nurtured and given a chance for survival.

Booking the Theatre

Fortunately for me, I have a name that people recognize—a brand. So it's a bit easier for me to get a cinema to play my films. I call up all of the theatres that I've worked with in the past. The theatre bookers usually know me by now, or know of me, and are willing to talk about scheduling a screening. I try to get a 50/50 split of the door, but sometimes that's very difficult, especially in the high-demand markets like New York and Los Angeles. So it's usually 60/40 or 70/30, with the theatre getting the bigger slice.

IDIOTS AND ANGELS POSTER (2008)

Next, I make press material, like postcards and posters, with information about all of the prestigious festivals the film has played at, and all of the awards it's won, by way of trying to show that my film is a huge hit. I'll also include any great quotes from press or celebrities. The postcards are relatively cheap, but the one-sheet posters are not, so I try to limit the number to around 100—remember, I'm paying for them out of my own pocket.

I then must make trailers, which is kind of fun. I love making trailers, because it's like making a music video—finding the best scenes from the film and shaping them into a little scenario that's about a minute long—then we duplicate it and mail copies out to the cinemas. Sometimes I send 35 mm trailers, or DVDs, depending on the systems available.

Of course, all of the reviewers have to get screeners and press kits, which is another expense. Be sure to add "Property of so-and-so" to the screeners as a watermark, or the film will end up all over the internet.

Personal Touch

But I think the most important aspect for me of self-distributing my films is making an appearance at the screening. When discovering a new film, nothing is more exciting for the audience than meeting the creator behind the film. I like to talk about how I created the film, wrote the story, built the budget, and made the artwork—the audience feels like they've become part of the creative process. They're involved in the movie industry! I also give everyone in the audience a quick sketch on the back of a postcard as a keepsake. My contact information is also on that card, so they can find out more about me and my films online.

Nontheatrical

Besides the art-house theatres and the occasional multiplex, there's also nontheatrical distribution, which includes screenings at museums, schools, corporations, and airlines. This market used to be much larger, but with the advent of DVD, these institutions can now get their films at a much cheaper price.

But you might get some screenings this way; again, you'll need your posters, postcards, and press materials.

Press Agent

Both theatrical and nontheatrical screenings are highly dependent on press, so it's important to get a press agent at this stage. Again, ask other filmmakers to recommend someone who understands indie film and animation, because those are both specialized areas.

Hopefully, your press agent has connections to all of the media—radio, TV, magazines, internet—and can line you up with lots of interviews to promote your screenings. Be sure to bring samples of your work, both original art and video clips on DVD. Also, I like to bring my postcards and give everyone on the crew a free drawing—they all get very excited about that.

That's happened to me numerous times. More often than not, they want to discuss computer animation, because that is the prevalent form of animation now. I just change the subject and talk about what I want to discuss. The interviewer may get angry or feel insulted. Tough titties: air time is precious. I want to get people to come to my show, not promote the latest Pixar film. Also, sometimes a little conflict makes the interview more interesting for the audience.

Guerilla Publicity

"TEAM IDIOTS," MY STREET PUBLICITY GROUP (2010)

When we were promoting *Idiots and Angels*, we got into street teams organized by Alexia Anastasio, the director of a documentary about me called *Adventures in Plymptoons*.

Fortunately, I have a lot of fans in the art schools here in NYC, so we recruited about 20 or 30 kids, gave them cool T-shirts ("Team Idiots") and some of my DVDs (I had no money to pay them) and asked them to put up posters in stores all around the neighborhood near the theatre where the film was playing. Then they'd ask the proprietor of the bar, club, or shop to pose with the poster in their window, and we put those photos up on the film's website for further publicity.

Viral marketing is another very useful avenue for getting the word out. I created a little 30-second animated piece from some scenes from *Idiots and Angels*—it was the scene with Angel mooning the airplane passengers, but I added a shot (not from the film) where the passengers mooned back at him. Then we ended it with a tagline: "Don't be an asshole. See *Idiots and Angels* at the IFC Cinema" and posted it on YouTube.

VIRAL YOUTUBE ANIMATION (2010)

It's very important these days to have a presence on the internet. More and more people are plugged into Facebook, YouTube, Twitter, and various blogs. I'm not so good at tweeting; I've tried it but I still don't have the hang of it. I do blog regularly, though, and I have a substantial following at ScribbleJunkies .com, a site I share with animator Pat Smith.

Facebook has been very helpful to me, as has posting clips of my animation on my YouTube channel. On my own website, http://plymptoons.com, my assistants post my appearance schedule and a schedule of where my films will be screened around the world. But I'm sure that by the time this book comes out, there will be more new opportunities on the web to help spread the word about festival screenings and other events.

But probably the best tool we used was the personal appearances. I committed myself to going to all of the art schools in NYC to talk about the film. I went to SVA, Parsons, NYU, and Pratt, and after each presentation I told the students that if their class went to see my film, I could get them a discounted rate. So for a number of nights, we had packed houses full of art and animation students.

TV Spots

We did talk about taking out ads in the newspaper, but at all my screenings I would ask people how they heard about my show, and 80 percent of them found out about it from the internet—a few from newspaper articles.

For *Hair High,* I actually bought some 30-second TV spots on Cartoon Network's *Adult Swim.* It was very prestigious to have those ads, and they were fairly inexpensive—I think $1,000 for NYC. But not a lot of people showed up for my premiere because of the TV spots.

If I ever get more money, I'd like to try a bigger TV campaign. Hey, maybe I'll compete with the big studios!

Television

Perhaps the biggest source of revenue from my films comes from television. I have three agents that sell my films to TV. Sydney Neter of SND Films sells my short films all over the world; he goes to all of the film markets, festivals, and conventions having to do with animation and TV.

Fortunately, I've built up such a name over the years that often the TV channels will buy the film sight unseen because they know I make a good product, and their viewers want to see my latest work.

It's ironic that although I consider myself a very American filmmaker, my films are more popular in other countries, especially in Korea, Russia, Spain, Germany, and France, than they are in the United States.

I've never understood why the French are so enamored with my films—it may have to do with E.D. Distribution, which has been handling my films there since the late 1990s. They've been able to build a huge audience for my work. I believe the French audience likes the idea that I do work with adult sensibilities—sex, violence, love, and humor. As you may know, the mature graphic novel was a big phenomenon in France long before it became popular here. I'm hoping that soon adult animation will become more popular here, like it already is in France. Also, the French appreciate the fact that I'm an "auteur"—that is, I'm outside of the Hollywood corporate system and I make my films (almost) totally single-handedly.

Thanks to E.D. Distribution, Canal Plus, and Arté, a lot of my revenue comes from France.

In other markets, my features are represented by Catherine Branscome. She also goes to all of the film markets to make sales for my features, all over the world.

It seems like every country on the planet has a public TV station that shows short films—sometimes it's just as filler between the newscasts or feature films, and they all want product that is funny and universal. And that's why my films sell all over the world—they're not dialogue-driven (so there's no need to translate them), they're short (five minutes or less), and they're funny. That's what the world wants.

If you don't believe me, go to YouTube—what are the clips that get the most hits? The ones that make you laugh. It's not the serious, philosophical shorts or the abstract ones, or the ones where some guy is baring his soul to the world—unless, of course, the guy is really weird, and then it's funny.

Although some of these foreign TV stations don't pay a lot, if there are enough countries buying the film, it adds up. And these sales to TV are what really keep my studio going and self-supportive.

Ownership

Animation has a special timelessness that keeps the value of the film very high; that's why I demand to retain ownership of my films. If you believe in your film—if you spend two years making it, and it represents all of your ideas, blood, sweat, and tears—then I would think you'd want to retain ownership and reap the rewards.

All you have to do is put a "©" symbol with the year and your name on the film itself, and then send a copy to the US Copyright office along with a filled-out form and a fee, and you're protected until the day you die—the film is 100 percent yours.

It's something I discovered when I first created "Your Face"—all of the buyers asked me, "Who owns the film? Who is the producer?" Because that's the individual who gets the money and the prizes, not the director. So always be sure to insist on being the producer—along with getting that title in the credits.

Mini-Disney

I'll let you in on my little plan—since I started making animation in 1985, I've amassed quite a library of films, over 40 shorts and 9 feature films, and I try to keep all of my work in circulation. In other words, the more my films screen around the world, the more money I take in, and the more films I can make in the future. And hopefully my films will get better and better, because I'll have more money to invest in them. Plus, I believe I'm learning more and more about the trade of animation, so the quality gets better, too.

In fact, I'm starting to consider myself a mini-Disney studio of sorts. Disney started out making shorts, then moved into features, and eventually had enough films to have his own TV show and his own network. Now, don't start expecting to see a "PlymptoonsWorld" in your neighborhood anytime soon, but Disney definitely showed me the way to be self-sufficient and retain control of all my work, so "thanks, Walt!"

A few years ago, while attending the San Diego Comic-Con, someone handed me a piece of paper with the address of the "secret" Disney animation party. I thought this was really cool: I could sneak into their party and maybe meet a few real animators. So I sheepishly walked up to the door lady—she was hesitant to let me in, but fortunately I knew someone inside and she let me pass. So there I was in heaven—all these artists who made the great Disney films! But then something strange happened—I could hear this buzz going around the room. Uh oh: they'd discovered that I was an intruder, an imposter, and that I didn't belong there.

As I listened more closely, I could hear, "There's Bill Plympton!" and "Bill Plympton is here!," and then people started surrounding me, asking if I was really Bill Plympton—they all wanted to meet me! That was fine, but it seemed a little weird because I make these tiny indie films that no one sees, and these Disney artists make films that are seen around the world on 10,000 screens, with billboards everywhere—what the hell? They make millions a year and get health benefits.

In any case, I got a lot of free drinks and made a lot of friends that night. It seems they were amazed that I did all the drawings myself, and distributed my films myself, and made money!

DVD

DVDs are another wonderful source of income for me—they say DVD is a dying medium, so I guess we'll find out in a few years if that's true. I produce my own compilations, but my shorts are also included on other collections, like "Dogs on DVD" or "The Best of Anima Mundi." There are many DVD compilations made around the world, and my films fit in very well, because they're short, funny, and generally without dialogue.

Another great facet of DVDs is the extras. I get to include the pencil tests, documentaries, concept art, influences, photos, and the commentary track. So they become more than just a film on a disc—they become an educational and inspirational tool that is unequalled by any other medium.

Piracy

One of the big problems is piracy. Because animation is such a universal art form, my films have been pirated all over the world. I recently did a show in Moscow, and for some strange reason, I was mobbed everywhere I went. Even at my hotel, I had fans waiting to ambush me in the lobby. What was going on? My films rarely play on Russian TV—it had to be the black market! My films are all over the place on DVD and the internet. China's the same way—when I did a show there, I was violently mobbed by fans. But I've never sold my films to China; my works are way too raw for Chinese government sensors. So how did all those fans know my work?

There's talk of making piracy a much more serious crime—and I, for one, am all for it. I have a studio, I have employees, and I need to pay them. I need to pay my lab bills, and all my actors. If I can't get money coming in, I'm screwed; I'll have to shut down the studio and go into real estate like everyone else.

Even now, John, my office manager, spends a lot of time searching the web looking for sites that are showing my films without authorization. He usually sends them a polite form letter stating that if they don't take down my films, we'll have to take them to court.

But that in itself can be a full-time job. It's like fighting against the ocean. That's why I'm very hopeful that the government passes stricter anti-piracy laws.

VOD

Another source of income for me is the internet: iTunes, VOD (video on demand), and such. It's still fairly early to determine what will be the dominant vehicle for internet sales. Hell, maybe there will just be hundreds of different formats for selling cartoons! But I think for me, being independent and outside the Hollywood sphere, it will eventually become the best way to go. I foresee a day when I'll make my films and they'll go out immediately on the internet, and I'll receive (hopefully) fat royalty checks because of all of the millions of people around the world subscribing to my website.

Merchandise

Another great source of income for me is merchandise, another facet of the animation business fully developed by Mr. Disney. He realized that the audiences really connected with his characters and that people wanted to have a more intimate relationship with Mickey and his pals. So he began initiating and promoting merchandise, and it's become a huge source of income for both Disney and Pixar.

I've been able to take a lot of my early print cartoons and compile them into three books, which are a constant source of income. I also have posters, T-shirts, DVDs, music CDs, and original art. I'm now pursuing the possibility of creating little Guard

Dog dolls that we can market. The problem is that I don't usually have the time or money to concentrate on loads of merchandise—my love is drawing and creating the new film projects, and that keeps me pretty busy.

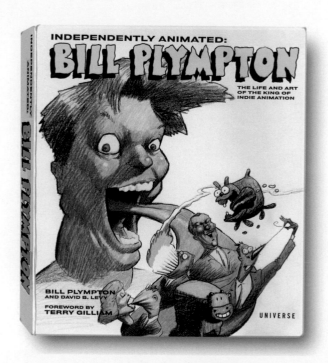

VARIOUS FORMS OF MERCHANDISE.

Personal Appearances

Making personal appearances—speaking at art schools, universities, museums, and conventions has become a larger aspect of my money-making efforts. Now that I'm much better known and I have an international reputation, I've found that I'm invited to speak at these special events, or hold "Master Classes." It's fun doing these appearances, and some of them pay pretty well.

In all modesty, I believe my Master Classes are great. They take about 1½ to 2 hours to perform, and I talk about my career as an indie animator who makes a living from short films. Then I show some of my classics, plus some brand new films, or works in progress. Then I like to show people how I draw, so I do demonstration sketches on a large art pad. I usually give away the drawings at the end of the show. Then there's a short Q&A session, and then everyone who comes gets a little cartoon drawn by me on the spot. I've been known to give sketches to 300 people each show.

This show has become quite popular; I've done it for the École des Beaux-Arts in Paris, at the great Annecy Animation Festival, and also for all of the big studios—Disney, Blue Sky, DreamWorks, Pixar, EA Games, and Lucasfilm.

However, one aspect of personal appearances that I really do not like is teaching students, which is quite different from lecturing. Dealing with animation classes drives me up the proverbial wall. These kids show me their films, some of which are pathetically flawed, and expect me to make them brilliant in a few moments. Hey, I have enough trouble making my own films entertaining. And these kids, who are obsessed with manga and animé, think their films are genius. So I have to tell them their shorts are crap, and they freak out. It really wears down my spirit. I have to either lie to them or crush their tender egos—that's why I don't like teaching, and that's why I'm writing this book. This is my animation class.

Commissioned Work

The final source of income is commissions. This aspect was very lucrative in the 1990s; I made a ton of money. I was the flavor of the decade.

But, within the last ten years, the commercial work has been dropping off. Either my work is over-exposed, or everyone now wants computer animation. Whatever the case, I only do one or two commercial jobs a year now.

For these jobs, my commercial agent, Ron Diamond of ACME Filmworks, usually sends me some storyboards that he's received from the client (advertising agency). He tells me the budget and when they need the spots. If I accept, I send in some sample frames (color sketches)—basically, how I visualize the ad following their boards. You must understand that the agency often sends out boards to numerous animation studios, and there are sometimes 20 artists bidding on the same campaign. So the odds of me getting the job are not so great. When I was a hotshot in the 1990s, they would often want me alone, and no one else would get the opportunity to bid. That was a sweet time, and I didn't realize how rare that was.

Now, of course, budgets are way down, and there's a lot more competition. But that's okay—I'm making good money on my shorts and features, so I'm not as reliant on commercials as I used to be.

Music Videos

"HEARD 'EM SAY," KANYE WEST MUSIC VIDEO (2005)

Back when I was working for MTV in the 1980s, music videos were the hot art form. The money was great and everybody was talking about them.

My first music video was a pitch I made to Madonna for "Who's That Girl?" I didn't get the gig, but I ended up doing the animation.

I've done videos for Peter Himmelman, Kanye West, Parson Brown, and two for my dear, wacky friend "Weird Al" Yankovic.

All my music video deals have come through agents, except Kanye's—he called me personally.

The budget can be anywhere from $10,000 to $500,000. I usually get the low end of the money tree, because I don't do computer graphics and I don't use live action.

Once I agree to take on a job, the artist sends the music and I give him or her back some storyboards. Usually, they accept my ideas and I have between two weeks and two months to finish. I generally take half the money up front and the second half upon delivery. The artist will usually accept the finished piece because of tight deadlines, but occasionally they'll ask for a few changes.

I love music videos because I'm free to experiment and try new ideas, and they're seen all over the world by billions of people. I like that!

Chapter 13

Advice to Young Animators

In 1990, when I started to create *The Tune*, I didn't really realize that I'd be ushering in a revolution in independent animation.

To me, it was quite an ordeal creating all of the drawings and hand-coloring each one. There must have been about 25,000 individual drawings.

Now, of course, kids can put together long animated films on their Macs. Anyone who knows Flash can make a feature film in their spare time. I think that's terrific! What this world needs is more animated films. In the first Golden Age, we'd be lucky to get one feature every three years; now, we get to see two or three new features a month. I love it! All those different ideas, techniques, and stories: I'm in heaven.

I've created a genre—Indie Animated Features.

Finding the Right School

If I were a young kid who loved animation, I'd do things very differently from the way I did them 40 years ago.

Do you have any career advice for students?

First of all, there are so many great film and animation schools today available for young film lovers. I can't recommend any specific school, because I never went to one, but here are some of the schools that seem to produce great talent:

School of Visual Arts in NYC

New York University

Parsons in NYC

Pratt in NYC

Rhode Island School of Design

Rochester Institute of Technology

Ringling College of Art and Design in Florida

Savannah College of Art in Georgia

Cal Arts in California

Chapman University in California

University of the Arts in Philadelphia, Pennsylvania

Sheridan Art School in Toronto, Canada

Vancouver Film School

Gobelins School of the Image in France

Supinfocom in France

Filmakademie Baden-Württemberg in Stuttgart, Germany

Each school has its pros and cons: do research on the Web and look at who graduated and what sorts of programs they emphasize. Do they have life drawing? What's the cost? Is it easy to find living space? Do they have any teachers you want to study with? You must balance all these qualifications before you make your decision.

What to Study in School

If I were running an animation school, these are the classes I would emphasize:

1. Drawing, lots of drawing (especially life-drawing)

2. Film and Art History

3. Illustration History (N. C. Wyeth, A. B. Frost, R. O. Blechman, Winsor McCay, Milton Glaser, Howard Pyle, Norman Rockwell, and others)

4. Design

5. Storyboards and Storytelling

6. Humor

7. Color Theory

8. All the software programs—Photoshop, Flash, Maya, and so on

9. Business of Art

Also, I recommend finding a great teacher or mentor. Of all the teachers I had in college, only two of them really taught me anything. I was lucky; some people go through school never connecting with someone to change their life and career. So search around for that inspirational figure, ask your friends, go on the Web—they're out there, and they may not be at your school. That's okay. If you find someone with a studio, be an intern—volunteer to work there for free so that you can suck up all the knowledge you can.

We often use interns in our studio; it works out well for both parties. We get help to put together our films, and the intern gains valuable knowledge about how the real world of indie animation works. Plus they get their name in a Bill Plympton film—that looks terrific on their resume.

Make a film in school—maybe two or three—but by all means, don't make them over two minutes. Two minutes is a perfect length—it's great for entering into festivals, and it's perfect to show as a portfolio piece or at interviews.

Please, please, *please*: do not make an epic film in college! A well-made two-minute short is so much better than a rushed, uncolored ten-minute film. I've seen way too many of those.

And please don't animate on ones—use threes or fours!

After School

You've graduated from art school; you have a very cool portfolio and a terrific two-minute short. Where do you go?

I suggest finding an animation studio, whether it's Pixar or Blue Sky or a tiny boutique studio like my own (or a games company, advertising agency, production company, or edit house) and starting from the bottom. Don't be shy; be bold! I found out too late that Ralph Bakshi was making his first feature, *Fritz the Cat,* in NYC the year I moved here. Damn, I'm kicking myself for not going to his studio and volunteering to help out. I could have learned so much, and I believe my animation career would have started 15 years earlier. C'est la vie.

Starting at a studio is like the sequel to art school; learn all the new programs. Make lots of friends in the business, as you'll be seeing them throughout your life in the industry. Put some money in the bank and build up your savings account. Start stockpiling ideas—lots of concepts, scripts, sketches, and storyboards. Polish your technique and drawing skills, and fill up your sketchbook.

After seven or eight years, you'll be ready to develop your own strong, unique style of art and storytelling. Strike out on your own—if you're insecure or not sure of your talents, you can keep your day job and make your indie film on the weekends. But, as Nike says, "Just do it."

I'm a mess of doubt. When people say they love my films, or when I get massive applause, are they trying to make me feel at home?

Are they applauding because I did all of the drawings myself?

Are they just trying to be polite?

Are they trying to be my best friends?

Or do they really like my film?

I don't know. I have no way of knowing. Maybe the organizers forced them to do that before I appeared? Did the organizers offer them money to pretend they liked my film? I don't know! People seem to like my films, but the distributors stay away like the plague.

Also, I don't know why there are large crowds at my screenings all over the world.

Is it because of my MTV exposure?

Word of mouth?

Is it because my films are on YouTube and the internet?

Or on pirated DVDs?

Did they pay people to come see my film? I don't know!

God, yes, tons of them. I'm not like Frank Sinatra, who sang "My Way," or Edith Piaf, who sang "Non, je ne regrette rien" (French for "I regret nothing"). I make a lot of big mistakes, and I'll probably make a lot more.

My biggest regret is that I didn't start making animation right out of college. Perhaps I could have been as big as Tim Burton or John Lasseter if I had trained as an animator and not an illustrator. But who knows?

I think that's why I'm in such a hurry, making two or three shorts a year and a feature every two or three years—I want to make up that 15 years of lost time that I spent as an illustrator.

It's amazing; I have that same yearning I had as a kid when I got my little notepad. I still want to draw everyone's face, and everything in the world around me. And I hope I never lose that love of drawing.

What's your next project?

I have a lot of ideas, all ready to turn into films, so it's tough to decide. But it will certainly be the project that's the most exciting and challenging.

Here are my top ten commandments for young animators:

1. Follow Plympton's Dogma.

2. See as many films as possible (shorts and features).

3. Keep an idea file.

4. Always carry a sketchpad.

5. Draw every day.

6. Create something that no one's seen before.

7. Beware of big egos: yours and other people's.

8. Be curious about life.

9. Appreciate the humor in life.

10. Love what you do.

AFTERWORD

I know a lot of artists who have very exotic, rare types of brushes, or pencils that can be ordered only from special shops or only from the factories at a very premium price.

But not me: I like the good, old standard—a Ticonderoga #2 pencil. It's the utensil I first used as a kid—perhaps that's why I love it. It takes me back to my first discovery of drawing at the age of 4.

There's a very special relationship that develops between my Ticonderoga #2 and me. I get them in a green pack of 12. I've discovered that they're very fragile when they're new—if I drop one on the floor, sometimes the lead inside will fracture, and then it becomes very difficult to sharpen to a fine point without the lead falling out.

As each #2 pencil begins its life cycle, it starts out as just another drawing device, yet over the many drawn lines, I begin to bond with this lovely creature. We're like partners in the creative act. I give her a nudge, and magically she creates these amazing visions.

And if either of us makes a mistake, we only have to invert her and rub her derrière on the paper, and voilà—we're good to go again.

As the days and drawings wind by, I can feel her getting smaller in my hand—each time I put her into the sharpener, it's like I'm cutting off my own arm. I almost break out in tears as I whittle her down to just a fraction of her former beautiful self. But, in spite of her now-shortened state, she still performs magnificently—keeping a nice, smooth line, filling in the crosshatching. I can feel her confidence as we work together like a pair of champion ice skaters.

We feel comfortable in each other's arms, but sadly, it's become the autumn of her life. She knows I will abandon her and move on to a new lover. Alas, that's what the art world is like—it's a cruel business.

Oh, yes, I can get a pencil holder to prolong our relationship. But even that is a signal that our time together is nearing its sad end—the sorrow of when I say "au revoir" to my beloved #2. We've had a lot of crazy, fun adventures together. She was my fabulous muse, a veritable font of creative ideas, but now she's just a nubbin. As I drop the stub into my wastebasket and wave goodbye, I think of the wonderful times we had together—the great art that we produced—a tear comes to my eye and she bounces sadly on the bottom of the basket.

I turn my head away—oooh, there's a nice new young Ticonderoga #2 beckoning me to grab her, fondle her, and make wonderful, artistic love all day long. Am I cheating on my lover so soon?

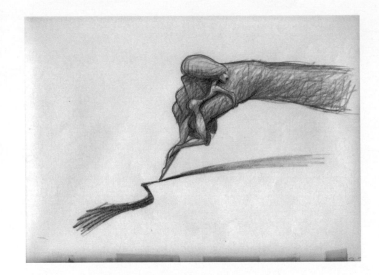

INDEX

Note: Page numbers followed by *f* indicate figures.

A

Animation
  art digitizing
    cleaning, 159
    color, 159–160
    compositing, 160–161
    scanning, 158–159
  art finishing, 153–158
  backgrounds, 150–151
  caricatures
    character and movement, 117–120
    drawing's reflection, 120
    emotions and personality, 121
    exaggeration, 116, 120
    facial features, 117
    Grossman, Robert, 116
    human face, 116
    Levine, David, 116
    line of action, human body, 117
    McGillivray, Bruce, 116
    unique and compelling shape, 116*f*
    verbal description, face, 120
  cel animation, 112
  character design (*see* Character design)
  claymation, 112
  collage, 113
  computer graphics, 112
  2D drawing style, 113
  design, 132–133
  distortion, 143–144
  drawn animation, 112
  early influences (*see* Early influences)
  face
    Burke, Philip, 131
    cheeks and jaw, 128, 130*f*
    directional signals, 132
    emotion and personality, 125
    eyes, 126, 126*f*, 127*f*
    female, 131, 131*f*
    human head, 131, 132*f*
    mouth, 127, 128, 129*f*, 130*f*
    noses, 126, 127, 129*f*
    teeth, 128
    "The Tune," 131
    "The Wiscman," 131, 131*f*
  film making (*see* Film making)
  finger on fogged glass, 113
  flash, 112
  golden age (*see* Golden age)
  human body

Animation *(Continued)*
    animé, 121
    bones, 125, 125*f*
    clothing, 122–123, 122*f*
    feet, 122, 122*f*
    hands, 124, 124*f*, 125
    Japanese manga art., 121
    ugly drawings, 121
  influences
    Back, Frédéric, 111
    Blair, Preston, 111
    de Wit, Michael Dudok, 111
    Kahl, Milt, 111
    Keane, Glen, 111
    McCay, Winsor, 110–111
    Miyazaki, Hayao, 111
    Quinn, Joanna, 111
    Scribner, Rod, 111
    soul characters, 112
  metamorphosis, 145–146
  mixed media, 113
  money *(see* Money making)
  multitude style options, 112
  oil on glass, 112
  paper/cut-out, 112
  pencil test, 146–150
  perfectionism, 152–153
  perspective and foreshortening, 140–143
  pin screen, 113
  point of view, 138–139
  postproduction *(see* Postproduction)
  previz, 135–137
  puppetry, 112
  sand painting, 113
  secrets, 113–115
  self-distribution *(see* Self-distribution)
  shadows, 144–145
  silhouettes, 134–135
  stop-motion, 112
  story telling *(see* Story telling)
  textures, 113*f*
  voices *(see* Voices)
  walk cycles, 137

Association Internationale du Film
  d'Animation (ASIFA)
  Annie Awards, 192–193
  screening in New York, 199–200

C

Caricatures
  character and movement, 117–120
  drawing's reflection, 120
  emotions and personality, 121
  exaggeration, 116, 120
  facial features, 117
  Grossman, Robert, 116
  human face, 116
  Levine, David, 116
  line of action, human body, 117
  McGillivray, Bruce, 116
  unique and compelling shape, 116*f*
  verbal description, face, 120

Cartoonal knowledge, 17

Casting
  character personality, 105
  film festivals, 104
  "Hair High," 101–102, 103, 104
  "Idiots and Angels," 104
  Long, Justin, 102
  "Mutant Aliens," 101–102
  non-SAG voice actors, 105
  pencil test, 106
  Perry, Matthew, 103
  Plimpton, Martha, 102*f*, 103
  reference footage, 107
  SAG, 101, 102
  Showalter, Michael, 102
  sound designer, 101
  sound engineers, 101, 106
  "Tiffany," 104
  voice-over sessions, 107
  voice-record session, 106

Cel animation, 112

Central park sketch, 16*f*

Character design
  architectural, 87*f*
  car designs, 88*f*
  dynamic shapes, 77–79
  of EL MERTO, 84*f*
  evolution of, 82*f*
  extreme acceptable facial
    characteristics, 90*f*
  of HITMAN, 86*f*
  of Jake, 83*f*
  life-drawing, 74
  line of action, 80–88
  miscellaneous, 85*f*
  pushing the eye around, 89–90
  simplicity, 79
  strong personality, 77
  top no-nos, 91
Claymation, 112
Collage, 113
Color
  art digitizing, 159–160
  art finishing, 153–158
Computer graphics, 112

D

Dolby, 175
Drawn animation, 112

E

Early influences
  Addams, Charles, 11
  Disney and MGM cartoons, 9–10
  Disney feature, 10
  electronic media, 8
  illustrator, 9
  photographic memory, 8
  Preston Blair book, 9–10, 10*f*
  sick humor/dark humor, 11
  studio's income, 8
  Walt Disney entertainer, 8
  Warner Bros, 11

F

Fame and fortune schedule, 17
Film making, 17
  alternative funding
    funding ideas, 44
    marketing and animation
      techniques, 44
    product promotion stunts, 44–45
  animation business, 24
  gap model, 25*f*
  Plympton's dogma
    cheap film, 41

  funny film, 41–43
  shot film, 40–41
  procedure, 24
  raising money
    budget, 28–30
    cartoon city, 26
    concept art, 34
    daydream, 26
    family and friends, 36
    grants, 35–36
    GTFM, 25
    "Guard Dog," 26
    hollywood, 36–37
    idea/concept, 25
    kickstarter and internet, 37–38
    marketing plan (*see* Marketing plan)
    receptive, 26
    self-investment, 39–40
    synopsis/storyboard, 27–28
    title, 35
    visual/paragraph, 27
Flash, 112

G

Get the friggin money (GTFM), 26
Golden age
  animated cartoons explosion, 4

Golden age *(Continued)*
   animation jobs, 3
   animation production funds, 4
   audience, 4
   characters, 2–3
   gourmets, 5
   grossing films, 4
   Hanna-Barbera and Rankin/Bass series, 3
   Japanese animation, 3–4
   MTV logo, 3*f*
   needs, 5
   pencil, 6
   Pixar, 5

H

Hamptons beach mansion, 18
Hues, 156

I

Intuition, 55–56
Ironic music, 177–178

J

Japanese manga art, 121
Jarmusch, Jim (filmmaker), 20

L

Lee, Spike (filmmaker), 20

M

Marketing plan
   audience importance, 33
   distribution companies, 30
   festival circuit, 30
   painting styles, 33
   profit, 30
   Tarantino of animation, 32
Metamorphosis, 145–146
Money making, film
   comic conventions, 198–199
   distribution deal, 205–206
   distributor complaints, 206–208
   market festival
      American Film Institute festival, 195
      Animafest Zagreb, 195
      Animator festival, 195
      Annecy, 191–192
      Annie Awards, 192–193
      Aspen Shorts festival, 195
      Bibliotheque (library), 193
      Cannes, 191
      Clermont-Ferrand, 193

      Deauville American Film Festival, 194
      Expression en Corto, 193–194
      Fantasia festival, 195
      fun, 196–198
      Göteburg festival, 195
      Hong Kong Film Festival, 195
      internet, 199
      Korean festivals, 195
      nominal fee, 199
      Oscar-nominated, 191
      Ottawa Animation Festival, 193
      Palm Springs Shorts Festival, 194
      posters, 201
      press agent, 200
      press fee, 200
      press packets, 200
      screening fee, 200
      Sitges, 194
      star characters drawing, 201
      Stuttgart Animation Festival, 193
      Sundance, 191
      Toronto Worldwide Shorts
         Festival, 194
      Tribeca Film Festival, 194
   MTV animation, 190
   strange person deal, 203–204
   telluride story, 204–205
   tune deal, 202–203
   Your Face, 190

Music, 172*f*
- budgeting, 178–179
- clearances, 184–185
- film composers, 183–184
- "Idiots and Angels," 177, 177*f*, 179–181, 182
- ironic music, 177–178
- McElheron, Maureen, 176
- saving money, 179–183
- "Your Face," 176

O

Oregon's climate
- cartoonists and animators, 13
- Chinese water tortures, 12
- classmate, 14*f*
- Elvis cartoon, 15*f*
- natural phenomena, 13
- pencil drawing, 15*f*
- radiograph drawing, 15*f*
- rainfall and rainstorms, 12
- school cartoon, 13*f*, 14*f*
- watercolor, 14*f*

P

Paper/cut-out, 112

Perfectionism, 152–153

Pin screen, 113

Plympton's dogma
- cheap film, 41
- funny film, 41–43
- shot film, 40–41

Point of view (POV), 138–139

Postproduction
- conflict, 167
- Dolby, 175
- editing, 164–165
- effects, 168–169
- film review, 172
- humor, 169–170
- music, 172*f*
  - budgeting, 178–179
  - clearances, 184–185
  - film composers, 183–184
  - "Idiots and Angels," 177, 177*f*
  - ironic music, 177–178
  - McElheron, Maureen, 176
  - saving money, 179–183
  - "Your Face," 176
- real *vs.* real cartoony sound, 174–175
- sound, 172–174
- testing, 185–187
- timing
  - caricature making, 167

"Idiots and Angels." 165–167, 165*f*, 166*f*
- quick cuts, 165
- Shane Acker film 9, 165
- tempo exaggeration, 167

Previz, 135–137

Print cartoons, 18–20

Production
- animation business, 50
- festivals and speaking engagements, 50
- good and bad employees, 49
- pencil test, 50
- Plymptoon's studio, 51*f*
- studio creation, 48–50

Puppetry, 112

Purple concept, 16

S

Sand painting, 113

School humor
- class artist, 11
- grade school drawing, 11, 11*f*
- "independent short," 12
- school newspaper, 12
- school poster contest, 12*f*

Screen Actors Guild (SAG), 101, 102

Self-distribution
    commissioned work, 222
    DVD, 217
    Guerilla publicity, 212–214
    merchandise, 219
    mini-disney, 216–217
    music videos, 223–224
    nontheatrical, 211–212
    ownership, 216
    personal appearances, 221
    personal touch, 211
    piracy, 218
    press agent, 212
    television, 214–215
    theatre booking, 210–211
    TV spots, 214
    VOD, 218–219
Shadows, 144–145
Silhouettes, 134–135
Stop-motion, 112
Storyboarding
    animatic, 94
    decisions, 94
    development/transformation, 96
    essential animatic, 96
    individual shots, 96
    story reels, 96
    thumbnail sketches, 94–96

Storytelling
    censorship *vs.* self-censorship,
        71–72
    character development, 66–67
    children *vs.* adults
        children's cartoon avoidance, 68
        gratification, 69
        sex, 69
        violence, 69–70
    comedy
        conflict and contrast, 65
        contradiction, 65
        exaggeration, 65
        god-like power, 62
        guard dog, 62
        juxtaposition, 64
        personal pain, 65–66
        puns, 63
        reversing clichés, 64
        sex and violence, 63–64
        surrealism, 62
        tragic story, 63
    conflict, 57–58
    Hertzfeldt, Don (Rejected, Billy's
        Balloon), 58
    intuition, 55–56
    live action *vs.* animation, 70–71
    Lord, Peter (Aardman's Chicken
        Run), 58

    myth of story, 54–55
    Smith, Pat (Mask Delivery)
        action, 59
        animation, 59
        concentration, 61
        critics, 60
        festivals, 60
        goals, 61
        good ending, 58–59
        laughter quotient, 61
        own personality and emotion,
            61
        simplicity, 59
        subtle actions, 60
Strong personality, 77

U

Unpublished rapidograph
    illustration, 19*f*

V

Voices
    character personality, 105
    dialog, 100–101
    film festivals, 104
    "Hair High," 101–102, 103, 104

"Idiots and Angels," 104
Long, Justin, 102
"Mutant Aliens," 101–102
non-SAG voice actors, 105
pencil test, 106
Perry, Matthew, 103
Plimpton, Martha, 102*f*, 103
reference footage, 107
SAG, 101, 102
Showalter, Michael, 102
sound designer, 101
sound engineers, 101, 106
"Tiffany," 104

voice-over sessions, 107
voice-record session, 106

Y

Young animators
  after school, 228–229
  classes, 227
  film making, schools, 228
  great teacher/mentor, 227–228
  interns, 228
  right school, 226–227

two-minute short film, 228
"Your face" film
  Annecy, 21
  ASIFA competition screening, 21
  bizarre and humorous shapes,
    20–21
  colored pencil, 22*f*
  Jarmusch, Jim (filmmaker), 20
  Lee, Spike (filmmaker), 20
  MTV animation department,
    21–22
  MTV Movie Awards, 21–22
  Oscar nomination, 21

Printed and bound by CPI Group (UK) Ltd, Croydon, CR0 4YY

21/10/2024

01777115-0001